W9-BQH-243

DATE DUE

DEMCO 128-8155

MOUNTAINS IN THE SEA

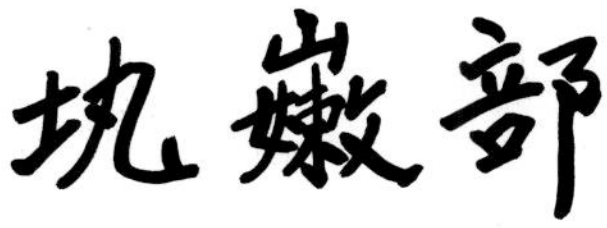

MOUNTAINS IN THE SEA

The Vietnamese Miniature Landscape Art
of Hòn Non Bộ

PHAN VĂN LÍT
with LEW BULLER

TIMBER PRESS
Portland, Oregon

All photographs by Lew Buller unless otherwise noted.
Frontispiece: Hòn Non Bộ by Phan Văn Lít called Sương Mai (A Foggy Morning).

Mention of trademark, proprietary product, or vendor does not constitute a guarantee
or warranty of the product by the publisher or authors and does not imply its approval
to the exclusion of other products or vendors.

Published in 2001 by Timber Press, Inc.
The Haseltine Building
133 S.W. Second Avenue, Suite 450
Portland, Oregon 97204-3527, U.S.A.

Printed in Hong Kong

Library of Congress Cataloging-in-Publication Data

Phan, Văn Lít.
    Mountains in the sea : the Vietnamese landscape art of Hòn Non Bộ / Phan Văn Lít
with Lew Buller.
        p. cm.
    Includes index.
    ISBN 0-88192-515-2
    1. Hòn non bộ. I. Buller, Lew. II. Title.

SB433.5 .P44 2001
635.9'772—dc21
                                                                        2001027693

Contents

Preface 7

Acknowledgments 9

Introduction 11

A Note on Pronunciation 15

CHAPTER ONE   Scenic Areas and Landscapes in Việt Nam, 17

CHAPTER TWO   The Historical and Cultural Significance of Hòn Non Bộ, 37

CHAPTER THREE   Enjoying the Art of Miniature Landscapes, 63

CHAPTER FOUR   Creating a Hòn Non Bộ, 79

CHAPTER FIVE   Making a Shallow Container, 105

CHAPTER SIX   Common Errors in Building Hòn Non Bộ, 119

CHAPTER SEVEN   Trees on Hòn Non Bộ, 129

CHAPTER EIGHT   Adding to the Mountain, 141

CHAPTER NINE   Tiểu Cảnh, A Miniscene, 153

CHAPTER TEN   Tools, 169

CHAPTER ELEVEN Displaying Hòn Non Bộ, 177

CHAPTER TWELVE A Gallery of Hòn Non Bộ and Tiểu Cảnh, 195

Index 227

Preface

No one actually knows when Hòn Non Bộ, Vietnamese miniature landscape art, began, but creating a scenic landscape in miniature has been a special pastime, full of art and elegance, enjoyed by the Vietnamese people for hundreds of years. It is now being appreciated by Westerners as well.

The Vietnamese people fought against invaders from the north for more than a thousand years and had little time for recording history or preserving documents. As a result, very few books or reliable documents on Hòn Non Bộ exist. I have, however, compiled some articles and evidence to show that the Vietnamese people have had a centuries-long interest in copying nature in an artfully reduced scale, in vivid and creative ways. To some extent, this form of recreation is considered a creed, an activity with deep cultural meanings and associations.

In earlier centuries, descriptions of this artistic creed could rarely be found in written form for it had been passed on through practice and word of mouth. Depending on the regional dialect, four terms are used to describe this art: *Giả Sơn*, artificial mountain; *Non Bộ*, mountain set; *Núi Non Bộ*, miniature mountain; and *Hòn Non Bộ*, Vietnamese miniature landscape art. *Hòn Non Bộ* can be thought of as "mountains above, water below."

I had the honor of being a guest demonstrator at the November 1997 Golden State Bonsai Federation convention in San Diego, California, introducing this special art of the Vietnamese people to the people of California. Bonsai enthusiasts showed a great interest in this art, and I was very proud to be invited to demonstrate it for the first time in the United States. On 26 November 1997, I returned to Việt Nam to visit many landscapes, historical places, and places believed to have been the cradle of this art in the North, the Middle, and the South.

This book is a collection of experiences, my own and others,' past and present, compiled from rare books, articles, lectures, presentations, and interviews with old-timers and experienced people. We offer this collection in the hope that the reader will also enjoy the art of Hòn Non Bộ.

I express special thanks to my wife and my gratitude to all scholars and friends who have given me invaluable ideas and encouragement to complete this work. I hope to hear comments and suggestions from readers to help me make it better.

PHAN VĂN LÍT
La Mesa, California

Acknowledgments

THE PLEASURE OF EXPRESSING our appreciation to the people who have helped us along the way falls to me. The list is short; the people are important.

First is Margaret Gingrich, PH.D., who spent weekends and holidays making two editorial reviews of our material. As a result of her work, our words will make more sense to readers. Our Vietnamese readers will enjoy the work of Trần Ngọc Dũng, who translated the poetry and other Vietnamese reference material from the original Vietnamese into English, and they will understand the importance of Chau Cheng Lim, who translated old Vietnamese materials written in Chinese characters, the method used before the Vietnamese adapted Romanized letters to their language.

Two publishers of bonsai magazines early on recognized Lít Phan's artistry and encouraged the continuation of his work. William N. Valavanis saw Lít Phan at work at the Golden State Bonsai Federation convention in San Diego, California, and encouraged him to produce an article, "Hòn Non Bộ," in *International Bonsai* (1998, no. 2). W. John Palmer, publisher of *Bonsai Today*, reviewed an early draft of the manuscript, gave his honest opinion that the pictures in that draft left something to be desired, and stirred us to go back and do a better job.

Paul Seiley created a web site, scanned in pictures and text, and referred interested viewers to us by e-mail. Giỏi Smith-Nguyễn, M.D., taught Lít Phan's wife, Mai, how to make the egrets that appear in many of the pictures of Hòn Non Bộ.

Two bonsai artists, Ernie Kuo, from whom I took lessons for three and a half years, and Kathy Shaner, who gives me a lesson every time I talk to her, helped me develop the technical skills to train and wire trees and the outlook necessary to create a work of living art.

Neal Maillet, executive editor at Timber Press, never knew how much pleasure and excitement he created for Lít Phan and me when he said he would publish our book.

My thanks go to my son, Steven, who lent me photographic equipment and encouragement, and to my loving wife, Martha, who was essentially a widow for the two years it took to write and photograph this book.

Lewis C. (Lew) Buller, ph.d.
San Diego, California

Introduction

by
LEW BULLER

THROUGHOUT THE LONG SWEEP of history, stones have been objects of awe and fascination for people of many cultures. Used by artists and architects, they also have been revered as religious articles. Their endless variety of shapes, sizes, colors, and components have enabled the creation of such diverse items as the obelisks and pyramids of Egypt, the heads of Easter Island, the statue of David by Michelangelo, the Stonehenge of the Druids in England, and the aqueducts of ancient Rome.

Strength and hardness, characteristics valued by builders, were important symbolically in religion. Jesus baptized his disciple Simon as Simon Peter, meaning Simon the Rock. Shape and color were important to the shamans who carried magical stones in their medicine bags. Patterns were studied by soothsayers who cast stones to divine the future. Sheer size may have something to do with the fact that the Aborigines of Australia hold Ayers Rock to be sacred. Natural beauty may have caused the early Japanese to believe that stones had souls and that cutting a stone allowed its spirit to escape. For these and many other reasons, stones have been venerated.

The ancient Vietnamese worshipped stones, believing them to hold magical powers. They also worshipped trees and rivers, and where the three objects were found together, the location had special importance. Other objects were also revered, but over the centuries, the living art of Hòn Non Bộ grew out of the worship of stones, trees, and rivers.

Similar living art forms developed in other cultures during the same time period. Because of commerce, immigration, and invasion, ideas were taken from one culture to another and so similarities as well as differences can be found in the living arts of each region. Penjing evolved in China, bonkei (a tray landscape in miniature using living and non-living material) reached a high level of art in Japan, and Hòn Non Bộ arose in Việt Nam. All can be considered tray landscapes or miniature landscapes in shallow containers, but each has its own special features. Hòn Non Bộ differs from the others in that it uses real water rather than sand or gravel to represent water, its landscape is always a mountain in the sea, and the tray is made of concrete rather than clay or marble.

The first few chapters of this book take the reader on a tour of Việt Nam to show the marvelous natural scenery that is the model for Hòn Non Bộ, to give a history of the development of Hòn Non Bộ throughout the different dynasties, and to express some of the philosophical and religious concepts that affected the evolution of the art and that differ from those of the Western world. The remaining chapters explain how to make Hòn Non Bộ with examples of each step of their creation, and show completed Hòn Non Bộ and Tiểu Cảnh from Lít Phan's collection.

This book is for two audiences. One audience is the large number of bonsai enthusiasts, both in the United States and abroad, who already have some understanding of the design, horticultural, and sculptural skills necessary to create miniature living landscapes. The other audience is the Vietnamese who have relocated to the United States and other countries, and especially their children. The children, many of whom will never have seen or cannot remember Việt Nam, will have an opportunity to see a part of its culture that has been important for thousands of years and is a part of their heritage.

In music, painting, and the other arts, there are individuals who stand out from the rest of the crowd because of their abilities and sometimes because they take the art in a new direction. Phan Văn Lít is one of those individuals, standing out because of his artistry, his dedication to wider recognition of Hòn Non Bộ as an art, and the changes he has made to the traditional forms. Over the years he has refined his sense of proportion, has added new features like waterfalls and mist to the landscapes, and has adapted to the use of nonVietnamese stones and plants. At any show where one of his creations is on display, you can find it easily because there will be a crowd around it admiring his work.

Even before he left Việt Nam, Lít had won awards for his horticultural skill. In 1980, he won the gold medal for his display of cactus and succulents at the National Show in Hà Nội. Considering that Việt Nam has a long monsoon season, growing cactus was not an easy feat. He continued his interest in cactus and succulents when he came to the United States in 1980, and by 1985 had won the blue ribbon at the Del Mar Fair for his display of succulents. Not the usual country fair, the Del Mar Fair goes on for nearly a month and attracts hundreds of thousands of people each year. For three years in a row (1986–1988), he won the award for excellence at the Los Angeles Arboretum for his display of succulents and Hòn Non Bộ. Afterwards, Lít was awarded permanent possession of the trophy.

As Lít had time and the opportunity to build Hòn Non Bộ in the United States, he decided that he would work to disseminate knowledge of this art as widely as he could. He started clubs where he taught the skills—how to work with plants, assemble stones, and make pots—to anyone interested, Vietnamese or not. He was instrumental in donating a Hòn Non Bộ to Balboa Park in San Diego. He has written articles for newspapers and magazines, done shows throughout southern California, and appeared at conventions of bonsai enthusiasts. In September 2000, he was a featured speaker at the International Bonsai Symposium held in Rochester, New York. In the United States, he is the pre-eminent Vietnamese-born practitioner of the art of Hòn Non Bộ.

Many topics mentioned in this book could be expanded and would be educational and interesting in themselves. A book can be only so big, however, and so the authors have had to make some decisions about what to include and what to exclude. A major decision was made to limit the amount of basic information on some topics. There are many good books on bonsai that will teach the beginner how to select, shape, grow, wire, and train bonsai—the very techniques used to develop plants for Hòn Non Bộ—and explain how to use the tools needed for the processes. Similarly, there are how-to-do-it books on woodworking and concrete working for the person who is interested in making concrete pots. The reader is asked to forgive these sins of omission and instead go on to enjoy the history of the art and to admire the artistry evident in the pictures.

A Word About Photography

Except for the pictures of scenes in Việt Nam, all pictures were taken with a Nikon F3 with a DA-2 sports viewfinder for easier framing. Most of the pictures, including the close-ups, were taken with a 55 mm micro-Nikkor. A 100-300 mm zoom-Nikkor with micro capabilities was used for a few close-ups; a 43-86 mm zoom-Nikkor was used for the remaining pictures.

After some experimentation with lighting, a set-up similar to that used for copying documents was chosen. While this occasionally resulted in some background shadows, the advantage of the even frontal lighting was that it could reveal the details in the compositions. Test this by looking at the picture on page 194.

A Note on Pronunciation

ALTHOUGH THE VIETNAMESE WORDS used in this book are written with the familiar letters of the Roman alphabet, the sounds attached to them are not the sounds familiar to people for whom English is their first language. Hòn Non Bộ is pronounced "hahng nahn bow," and the ending "g" in "hahng" is very soft, hardly audible. Tiểu Cảnh is pronounced "too khan."

The Vietnamese language is tonal and uses accent marks to show the correct intonations and therefore the correct meanings. For example:

Ha   the sound of laughter or the sound of exhaling
Hạ   to come down or descend; also summertime, depending on context
Hà   river
Há   open your mouth
Hả   open *or* what

Some words used later:

Hang	cave	"han" (the "g" is dropped and the "n" cut short)
Hoa Lư	a place name	"wa loo"
Hương	fragrant	"hoong"
Long	dragon	"laump" (with the "p" stopped or swallowed)
Sơn	mountain	"shun" (with the "n" barely heard)
Tử	children	"too"
Việt Nam	the country	"vee-ett nahm"

All Vietnamese words except proper names and place names have been translated as accurately as possible so the reader need not struggle with unfamiliar sounds. Inclusion of the original Vietnamese words is not meant to distract, but rather to let the Vietnamese reader, as well as the English-speaking reader, enjoy the book.

15

Hạ Long Bay in Quảng Ninh province,
North Việt Nam. Photo by Nguyệt-Mai Đinh.

Scenic Areas and Landscapes in Việt Nam

Favored by Mother Nature, Việt Nam is notable for a richness of naturally scenic places and landscapes, as illustrated in the folk expression
"a forest of gold and an ocean of silver."

Việt Nam, Old and New

Ancient Việt Nam was located in what is today the Henan province of China where
two famous places, Động Đình lake and the Nam Lĩnh mountain range, are well
known to many Vietnamese people. Having suffered from invasions and oppres-
sion by the northerners, the Lạc Việt—a former name for the Vietnamese—had to
emigrate south from this land of beauty, which is described by Phạm Văn Sơn in his
book of Vietnamese history, *Thời Thượng Cổ*:

> The range of Nam Lĩnh is so long and so huge that in the distance it looks
> like a dragon dancing in the clouds. The lake of Động Đình has a body of
> crystalline water. Wind skims over the surface of the lake, stirring up a thou-
> sand waves—one after another—that rush ashore. A good habitat for lively
> fishes and birds, the lake is a beautiful scene, added to by colorful wild
> flowers in bloom, making it a residence of Muses for the poet.[1]

The Việt Nam of today has the shape of an S, with China to the north and Laos
and Cambodia to the west. The north of Việt Nam contains many mountain ranges,
which together have the shape of many sickles arranged in fanlike form. The highest point in this area is the Fansipan, in the northwest. Separating Việt Nam from

Laos and Cambodia is a long mountain range called Trường Sơn, or Long Range Mountains, full of springs, high peaks, waterfalls, caverns, and precious trees—very inspiring for those interested in building Hòn Non Bộ. The south is an area of fertile plains and rich rivers and seas, with some small, low-peaked mountains; hence the landscape is not so varied there, except around Hà Tiên and Châu Đốc.

To the east, the East Sea, part of the Pacific Ocean, gives Việt Nam a long coastline—approximately 2025 miles (3260 km) from Mũi Ngọc cape in the north to Hà Tiên in the southwest on the Cambodian border—with many white sand beaches and rocky cliffs. The coastline is filled with beautiful scenery. A few of the many memorable landscapes from these different parts of Việt Nam are described and illustrated in this book.

Hạ Long Bay

A natural wonder of the world, Hạ Long Bay is a beautiful area near Cẩm Phả City, Quảng Ninh province, about 100 miles (160 km) from Hà Nội. Covering an area of 580 square miles (1500 square km), Hạ Long Bay has numerous small limestone mountains on about 1600 islands, of which 1000 or so have been named.

How did Hạ Long come to be? According to local legend, Hạ Long is the place where the Vietnamese people were saved from invaders by a herd of dragons that descended from the heavens. When an enemy fleet attacked the coast, the dragons arrived just in time to counterattack. During the counterattack, these dragons spit out thousands of pieces of diamonds. Each of the diamonds turned into an island or part of a solid wall to stop the advancing enemy. In the end, the invaders were defeated. When the war was over, the mother dragon did not want to return to the heavens. She decided to stay on earth with the Vietnamese instead. The place she chose to stay was then called Hạ Long (Dragon Descender); the place her dragon children descended was called Bái Tử Long (Dragon Children by the Shore). The tail of the dragon rested on an area called Bạch Long Vĩ (White Dragon's Tail), the isthmus of fine white sand of Trà Cổ.[2]

The name Hạ Long has existed for more than a thousand years, and it has inspired a great number of poets. Hạ Long Bay is a composition by Mother Nature, a landscape with amazing lines and shapes. Each mountain on the islands in the bay has its own mysterious atmosphere and appearance, such as Hòn Ông Lã Vọng, appearing as the figure of a person praying for luck and good weather; Hòn Đầu Người (Man's Head Island); Hòn Con Cóc (Frog Island); Hòn Con Rùa (Turtle Island); Hòn Con Chó (Dog Island); Hòn Gà Chọi (Fighting Cock Island); and so on.

The mountains and caves look like pieces of sculpture made by a genius. Names such as Hang Đầu Gỗ (Woodhead Cave), Hang Sửng Sốt (Astonishment Cave), Hang Trống (Drum Cave), Hang Trinh Nữ (Virgin Maid Cave), Hang Bồ Nâu (Brown Stork Cave), Hang Ba Hầm (Three Tunnel Cave), or Động Thiên Cung (Heavenly Palace Cavern), among others, refer to the specific shapes or statuelike silhouettes of the stalactite deposits in them, or to phenomena that the local people perceived as they came up with names for the caves. For instance, when people come into the Drum Cave, through its winding path under the gaps between rocks, they can hear drumlike sounds constantly resonating—probably from the wind blowing through the fissures of the rocks and creating an echo as the whistling sounds hit the walls of the cave. Some of the limestone deposits in the caves appear to be silhouettes of elephants, galloping horses, leaping tigers, herons, or statues like those of the emperor of heaven, god of thunder, god of birth, and god of death, or Avalokitesvara Buddha. They are very lively and pleasant to the eyes of the viewer.

Hòn Con Chó (Dog Island) in Hạ Long Bay.
Animal imagery is a favorite way of naming geographical features. Photo by Nguyệt-Mai Đinh.

19

Detail of Hòn Non Bộ by Lít Phan. With a little imagination, this could be named in a way that describes an American dog standing upright.

An island in Hạ Long Bay. The soft limestone is eroded not only by the waves but also by the mild acid rain that falls during monsoon season. Photo by Nguyệt-Mai Đinh.

Hương Sơn

In 1770, the Year of the Tiger, Hương Sơn (or Chùa Hương or Động Hương Tích) was designated by Lord Trịnh Sâm as the most beautiful of the three most beautiful caverns in north Việt Nam. Hương (fragrant) Sơn (mountain) is a limestone mountain located in the northeastern part of Hoà Bình province, a place where archaeologists have discovered remains of a Mesolithic civilization.

To reach Hương Sơn, one has to go upstream on the Swallow Spring from Bến Đục in Đục Khê village. The cruise is arduous because the watercourse is very winding, mostly between two steep rock cliffs, occasionally giving the feeling that rocks will block the way. When the boat approaches the rocks, however, the waterway is perfect. The water is so clear that weeds and cobbles are visible at the bottom. Along the shores of the stream are scattered thatched cottages and huts built against the rocky slopes of the mountains. Nearer to the cavern, the traveler can see hundreds of small limestone mountains in the shape of elephants kneeling side by side, as if they were all looking at something together. In legend, there were 100 of these "kneeling elephants," according to the natives of Hương Sơn. The elephants were supposed to kneel and listen to Buddha's teaching. For some reason, one of them turned its tail toward the Buddha. One of the Buddha's protectors hit this undisciplined elephant with his sword, striking off part of the animal's hip—and the scar is still there!

Many temples and pagodas are located in and around the cavern of Hương Tích, and the cavern has become the most attractive place in the area. Every lunar year, on the sixth of January, people from all corners gather there to celebrate what is called Chùa Hương Feast, using the phrase "đi Chùa Hương," a familiar expression that denotes this annual event. Going to Hương Sơn without visiting the cavern of Hương Tích would be lacking in forethought.

Travelers leaving the boat that has stopped at the foot of the mountain must climb an uphill path of about a mile and a quarter (2 km) before reaching the top. There the travelers, stopping to catch their breath, are welcomed by a sign written

Detail of Hòn Non Bộ by Lít Phan, boat by Nguyệt-Mai Đinh. This is a boat from South Việt Nam; it is somewhat pointed in front and has a shorter, slightly square back. Boats from central Việt Nam have long, sharply pointed prows and sterns; North Vietnamese boats have square prows and sterns similar to Chinese boats.

in Sino characters mounted on a stone gate. The entrance of the cavern, around which are green woods, opens wide like the mouth of a dragon. The cavern is very large and deep. From the mouth, a stone stairway of 120 steps leads to the floor of the cavern. In the middle of the floor, a huge stalactite hangs from the ceiling, touching the floor like a giant person pouring rice in the wind from a big basket, the image of Vietnamese women when they separate their good dry rice from debris (sand, rice hulls, leaves, straw, and so forth) before storing it away. This column was named Đụn Gạo (Rice Heap), although some call it Lưỡi Rồng (Dragon's Tongue).

Numerous smaller stalactites are present along the wall of the cavern, which in old times people imaginatively named Nong Tầm (A Fat Drying Basket of Silkworms), Né Kén (Cocoon Tip), Chuồng Lợn (Pig Pen), Ao Bèo (Hyacinth Pond), Cây Vàng (Gold Pillar), Cây Bạc (Silver Pillar), Đầu Cô (Girl's Head), Đầu Cậu (Boy's Head), and Cửu Long Tranh Châu (Nine Dragons Fighting for a Pearl). Young stalactite deposits drip percolating calcareous water—cool and sweet—that taps against the floor in interesting sounds. The dwellers called these water flows Sữa Mẹ (Mother's Milk).

Mountains and Yến Stream of Hương Tích Pagoda.
Yến, roughly translated, means "swallow," and it is the
name of a nearby village. Photo by Nguyệt-Mai Đinh.

23

Hoa Lư, The Ancient Capital City

The ancient capital of Hoa Lư is situated at Trường Yên village, Hoa Lư district, Ninh Bình province. It first became known in Vietnamese history in 968 A.D., when Đinh Bộ Lĩnh founded his capital of Việt Nam there, which was then called Đại Cồ Việt (Great Việt). (The various rulers founded their capitals wherever they pleased. More than one ruler may have chosen the same location for *his* capital.) In 984, Lê Hoàn expanded the capital, making it more and more magnificent. Many limestone mountains surround Hoa Lư, among which are beautiful scenes and caverns, including Tam Cốc, Bích Động, Thiên Tôn, Động Hoa Sơn, and Động Am Tiên. Traveling by boat, one cruises upstream on the Trường Yên river to enter these mountainous areas.

On the left shore of the Ghềnh Tháp river is a mountain, the peak of which projects over the course of the river. King Đinh Bộ Lĩnh is said to have stood on this promontory to observe military drills held in the area. Nearby is Động Am Tiên

Hoa Lư Mountain in Ninh Bình province. Note the shape of the tree and how it has been formed by its proximity to the mountain. Photo by Nguyệt-Mai Đinh.

(Fairy Temple Cavern), where it is said that tigers were raised by the king. Those who committed serious crimes would be thrown to the tigers for the beasts' meals.

To get to Động Am Tiên, one has to climb a stone stairway of sixty-two steps, then go along a narrow worn path across a vast valley used for rice cultivation. Surrounding the valley are high mountains with big trees and high cliffs. Here and there one can see temples or pagodas hidden in the thick foliage of the trees and bushes. After crossing the valley, one ascends 200 steps before reaching the entrance of the cavern. Not deep, but very large, the cavern's interior has many altars worshiping a great variety of Buddhas, deities, and fairies. Different sizes and shapes of stalactites hang from the ceiling, some of which are called the Buddha's hands, others lotus-in-bloom. Behind the altars, a narrow and deep tunnel runs to somewhere that no one has dared to explore.

From the entrance of the cavern, everything outside appears quiet and evergreen. The tranquil atmosphere calms visitors' minds and leaves them peaceful and carefree. Leaving Động Am Tiên, one continues the journey by boat upstream,

Hòn Chồng in Nha Trang province in Central Việt Nam. The combination of sparse vegetation, shallow sea, and an extended mountain forms an excellent model for Hòn Non Bộ. Photo by Nguyệt-Mai Đinh.

going through what is called Xuyên Thuỷ Động (Through-Water Cavern). The rock above the entrance to the cavern looks like a huge lizard whose legs are touching the water. Water has eroded much of the legs, leaving many hollows. Just inside the cavern it is very dark because the ceiling is close to the surface of the water. The farther in one goes, however, the higher the ceiling grows and the brighter the interior becomes. In the reflected light from the surface of the water, the stalactites are extremely beautiful. The dripping of percolating calcareous water resounds here and there like a hard rain.

Bích Động (Jade Cavern)

Bích Động (Jade Cavern) is known as the second most beautiful cavern in north Việt Nam after Hương Sơn. (The third most beautiful is Địch Lộng.) It is a scenic site in the Ngũ Nhạc Sơn mountain range in the hamlet of Đạm Khê, Ninh Hải village, Hoa Lư district of the Ninh Bình province. In front of the cavern is a large flat area called Tràng Thi embracing the winding river of Trường Yên. The cavern is in a mountain bearing the same name as the river. Bích Động is also the name of a pagoda, which has three different structures: Chùa Hạ ("infra pagoda") at the foot of the mountain; Chùa Trung ("mid pagoda") in the middle of the slope; and at the top, Chùa Thượng ("supra pagoda").

Moving from the infra pagoda, one sees that the mid pagoda has two parts. The front part is roofless, and the back is covered by the vault of the entrance to the cavern. Behind the main gate, twenty stone steps lead to a cave about 20 feet (6 m) high called the Dark Cave. Here, one must use a torch, and the light from the torch brightens up the cavern. One can see figures of heavenly creatures or animals on the wall: fairies, angels, gods and goddesses, dragons, turtles, eagles in flight, and tigers. It is so beautiful that nothing in the world could seem to match it. Looking out of the cavern, one can see a big rock that looks like a turtle and two big slabs of stone, which are very special. When tapped, the slabs emit sounds like those of the Vietnamese mõ, a hollow wooden gong, with one slab having a high tone and the other a low tone.

On the way up to Chùa Thượng, the supra pagoda, one can view the mid pagoda from above; it looks like a square windowpane. Chùa Thượng is a small structure near the top of the mountain from where one can see the peaks of the five-mountain range called Ngũ Nhạc (Five Musics).

The name Bích Động was given to these three pagodas by a high-ranking mandarin in the Lê dynasty, Nguyễn Nghiễm, who visited the site and was inspired by the beautiful scene. He had craftsmen inscribe the name on a flat piece of rock and hang it at the gate of the mid pagoda.

Ngũ Hành Sơn (Five-Element Mountain)

Ngũ Hành Sơn is a group of five mountains southeast of Đà Nẵng city, Quãng Nam province in central Việt Nam. From the weather station on top of Thủy Sơn (Aqua Mountain), the highest and biggest of the five, one can see Mộc Sơn (Wood Mountain). Kim Sơn (Metal Mountain) is the smallest and farthest from the station. Next to Mộc Sơn are Âm Hỏa Sơn and Dương Hỏa Sơn (Yin Fire and Yang Fire Mountain) and then Thổ Sơn (Earth Mountain).

Before King Gia Long won the struggle against Tây Sơn in the early 1800s, he hid himself in this area, and here a bonze, or Buddhist monk, taught him the way to unite the country. He did as he was told and succeeded. To show his gratitude, the king advised his successor to take good care of Ngũ Hành Sơn. In 1825, King Minh

Hang Gió Đông (East Wind Cave), Đà Nẵng. There is a West Wind cave that is also a naturally formed opening. Photo by Nguyệt-Mai Đinh.

Mạng came to the area and had it restored. He also named some of caverns there, such as Động Vân Thông (Nice Cloud in the Sky), Động Hoa Nghiêm (Solemn Beauty), Động Huyền Không (Dimming Space), and Động Thạch Nhũ (Stone Nipples). In the cavern of Thủy Sơn are two very beautiful caves called Hang Gió Đông (East Wind) and Hang Gió Tây (West Wind). People in Đà Nẵng called Ngũ Hành Sơn "Hòn Non Nước" (Mountain and Water). Hòn Non Nước is celebrated in folk poetry:

Quê em có dãi sông Hàn,
Có Hòn Non Nước, có hang Sơn Trà.

[My home village is beautified by the Hàn River,
The Hòn Non Nước and Sơn Trà caves hugging together.]

Hải Vân Pass

Besides the caverns and mountains, Việt Nam has many other landscapes worth seeing. One of these landscapes is Hải Vân Pass, which runs from the Trường Sơn (Long Mountains) to the sea. The pass, the top of which is almost always covered with fog, got its name because it is where one can see Hải (the sea) below and touch Vân (the clouds) above. The path through the pass is very winding and dangerous, with one side being rocky cliffs and the other deep chasms or gorges. Along the way, numerous waterfalls with torrential currents rush to the sea below. From the top of the pass, the sea is seen far away, deep blue, embracing the foot of the mountain. Waves strike against the rocky beaches, making long strips of white foam. The view is spectacular!

Đà Lạt Waterfalls

From Sài Gòn, there are two ways to reach Đà Lạt waterfalls. One can either go directly from Sài Gòn, which is the quickest route, or one can travel to Phan Rang (which is not far from Nha Trang where there are many white sand beaches worth seeing) before turning westward toward Đà Lạt. At Đà Lạt, there are many waterfalls such as Cam Ly, Prenn, and Liên Khương, which are not very high but which create a harmonious and peaceful environment that pleases the heart.

The Gouga Fall comes from a large lake that supplies all the water pouring down along a steep cliff, landing on the huge slabs of rock at the foot to create a boisterous, continual noise. In the morning sunlight, water vapor rising from the lake hangs a splendid rainbow over the fall.

Detail of Hòn Non Bộ by Lít Phan. The exquisite
sense of proportion keeps the viewer from realizing
the trees are less than 3 inches (7.5 cm) tall.

The Pon Gua Fall is stepped, and the amount of water running down these steps is so huge that the noise can be heard as far as 2 miles (3 km) away. Another beautiful stepped waterfall is Bản Giốc in Cao Bằng province in northwest Việt Nam. Waterfalls such as these have become the models for the waterfalls in modern Hòn Non Bộ.

Landscapes in Hà Tiên

Taking National Route 4 from Sài Gòn toward Hà Tiên, one crosses two rivers by ferry (the first at Mỹ Thuận and the second at Vàm Cống), a channel of the Mekong River, Sông Tiền (Fore River), by bridge, and the other channel, Sông Hậu (Hind River), by ferry again. Hà Tiên is a little town in Kiên Lương district, Kiên Giang province, on the border with Cambodia. The area includes many beautiful natural landscapes, with several limestone mountains along the coast and offshore, simi-

Detail of Hòn Non Bộ by Lít Phan. The isolated fishing hut and the bamboo bridge are common in Việt Nam. Here they are reproduced in miniature.

lar to those at Hạ Long Bay in the north. Unlike the high and sharp ridged mountains in north and central Việt Nam, these are not very high and mostly stand in isolation from one another.

Hà Tiên is notable for isolated, low mountain landscapes such as Đông Hồ, Tô Châu, Nam Phố, Thạch Động, Pháo Đài, and Đá Dựng, the capes of Mũi Nai and Bãi Dầu, the islands of Hòn Trẹm, and mountainous islands of Hòn Phụ Tử. The Hòn Phụ Tử mountains are about a third of a mile offshore from Chùa Hang (Pagoda Cave) beach. They are two mountains, but they look like two pillars of rocks, standing inclined in the direction of the waves rushing to shore. Surrounding these two pillars are numerous small slabs, which appear to fluctuate in the waves as if they were floating on the surface of the sea. At the foot of each pillar, all kinds of ivy and leafy plants huddle; there are no big trees.

According to ancient legend, nine monstrous animals lived in this region and killed many residents and local fishermen. One day two people, a father and his son, decided to get rid of the monsters. They fought bravely and killed seven of the monsters without any difficulty. But the remaining two were so strong and ferocious that the father and son had to summon all their energy for the fight. The beasts were finally killed, but the father and his son died from exhaustion afterward. Eventually, two pillarlike mountains appeared on the spot where they died. Viewed from the shore, the pillar on the right is in the shape of the father in standing position, and the pillar on the left is his son kneeling down with two hands clutched together, as if inviting his father to sit down. The love between the mythical father and son is everlasting.

Looking toward the shore from Hòn Phụ Tử, one can see a vast area full of small limestone mountains with uncountable caves and hollows eroded by the sea. Amidst these little mountains and close to the bay is a body of water that can only be reached when the tide is low. The view of this "lake" is outstanding, and its silent atmosphere brings chills to the spine.

In the middle of this salt-water lake is a fresh-water body called Giếng Tiên (Fairy Well). When King Gia Long was chased by Tây Sơn, he took shelter in this lake. Out of food and water, Gia Long and his men were about to die of hunger and thirst, but luckily he found this well, and he and his men were saved.

Offshore from Hà Tiên, to the southwest, is the island of Phú Quốc (Prosperous Nation), which is part of Kiên Giang province. Here, a spring called Suối Tranh (Thatch Spring) flows through gaps and fissures in rocks and ends in a waterfall with many steps. Though the fall is not high, the water pouring over the precipice looks like a gigantic strip of white silk magnificently hanging down from midmountain to the ground.

Hòn Phụ Tử (Father and Son Island), Hà Tiên in
South Việt Nam. Photo by Nguyệt-Mai Đinh.

Father and Son by Lít Phan. Feature for feature, this miniature landscape matches the original almost perfectly.

Detail of Hòn Non Bộ by Lít Phan. If the edge of
the pot did not show, the viewer would have no
way of knowing this is a miniature instead of a
full, natural landscape.

THE MANY SCENIC AREAS and beautiful landscapes of Việt Nam provide endless inspiration to those who love miniature landscape art. With sights like these surrounding the Vietnamese people, it is no wonder that the art of miniature landscape was developed and passed from generation to generation. Such beautiful natural scenes inspire people to build miniature copies of a jungle, a forest, a mountain, an island, or a mysterious cavern. These pieces of art can be placed at corners of the house or in front or back of it—even inside the living room, depending on the size and composition of the pieces. A miniature landscape is rewarding because, when feasting one's eyes on it, one feels at ease; all the worries of worldly life slip away for a moment.

Notes

1. Phạm Văn Sơn, *Việt Sử Tân Biên* (New Record of Vietnamese History), volume 1, Đại Nam, Glendale, California, 1956, p. 85.

2. Thi Sảnh, *Vinh Hạ Long Di Sản Thế Giới* (Hạ Long Bay, A World Heritage), Sở Thông Tin Quảng Ninh (Cultural and Information Service of Quảng Ninh Province), Việt Nam, 1995, p. 16.

Landscape in Hà Tiên, South Việt Nam. The sharp rise and fall of the mountains is recreated dramatically in various Hòn Non Bộ. Photo by Nguyệt-Mai Đinh.

CHINA

Cao Bằng

Phú Thọ
Hà Nội
Hòa Bình

Vịnh Hạ Long
(Hạ Long Bay)

Ninh Bình
Thanh
Hóa

Vịnh
Bắc Bộ
(Gulf of
the North)

LAOS

THAILAND

Huế
Đà Nẵng

VIỆT NAM

CAMBODIA

Nha Trang

Đà Lạt

Sài Gòn

Hà Tiên

Đảo Phú Quốc
(Phú Quốc Island)

Sông Cửu Long
(Nine Dragons River)

Biển Đông
(East Sea)

Mũi Cà Mau

35

Large Hòn Non Bộ in Đầm Sen Park, Sài Gòn,
South Việt Nam. Photo by Nguyệt-Mai Đinh.

The Historical and Cultural Significance of Hòn Non Bộ

Throughout Vietnamese history, Hòn Non Bộ have been built by emperors, kings, generals, and other important people as monuments, decorations, personal vistas, and cultural icons.

Philosophy of Hòn Non Bộ

Worship of Rivers, Trees, and Stones

For thousands of years, Southeast Asian people, especially the Vietnamese, have worshiped stones. They also prayed to spirits of rivers, trees, and mountains. Stones were placed next to ficus trees growing by rivers, and prayers were offered to the spirits of all three. The people also believed that mountain caves were homes to sacred spirits who built mansions in paradise to isolate their sacred world from the human world. By living near caves, the Vietnamese people made an effort to enter this sacred world so their souls would merge into the world of eternity.[1]

It was not always possible for people to live near a cave in the mountains, so in their own homes they created Hòn Non Bộ in containers with water and stones set together in such a way that they looked like mountain ranges with plants on them or like islands in the ocean. They also added figures of birds, animals, structures, and people.

Philosophy of Natural Heaven-Man-Earth

The Japanese apply the philosophy of Heaven-Man-Earth (a scalene triangle) to train their bonsai. "Heaven" is the top point of the triangle outlining the foliage;

"man" is the middle point; and "earth" is the lowest point of the triangle. The Vietnamese people also build their miniature landscapes based on this philosophy, with some differences. "Heaven" denotes the space above the miniature landscape, representing an invisible energy of nature—not, as in religion, God's or a superpower's domain. "Earth" is represented by the material world: rock, plants, and water. The third element, "man," may be the craftsman who builds the piece or the person who enjoys looking at it. (Although a few women today are beginning to create Hòn Non Bộ, it has traditionally been an art form created by men.)

ENGLISH	CHINESE	JAPANESE	VIETNAMESE
Heavens	天	天国	Thiên Nhiên (Nature)
Man	人	人間	Người (Man)
Earth	地	土地	Đất (Earth)

Professor Phan Quỳnh said in a presentation entitled "Philosophy of Hòn Non Bộ":

> If Heaven, Earth, and Man are considered the three main factors that can alter the universe, then Man should be the second most important one, for man has his own ability with boundless intelligence. Above man is space; under his feet is earth, which gives him things to survive. Hence, man has his own solid position in the universe as much as the other two factors.[2]

The Creed of Hòn Non Bộ

People in East and Southeast Asia lead different lives from Westerners, for they have a different outlook on life, a different way of thinking, and different aesthetic concepts. Tending to introversion, they prefer spiritual values. They follow creeds, the customs and traditions of the particular arts. Creeds to East and Southeast Asians mean the beliefs that lead one's thoughts and actions in doing anything, whether drinking wine, drinking tea, arranging flowers, creating bonsai or miniature landscape art, sword fighting, doing kung fu, enjoying music, playing chess, making verse, painting, and so forth. Creeds can be thought of as systems of beliefs, principles, or opinions that are accepted, believed, and held as being true.

The creed of Hòn Non Bộ does not have many rules and fine nuances, but rather is broad and general, emphasizing the proper relationship between heaven, earth, and man. In philosophy, Hòn, Non, and Bộ are individually revered, particularly when they are found together in a natural setting; in art they are united in a shallow basin. Uniting them in art is an old concept; at Hoa Lư in Ninh Bình province there are five Hòn Non Bộ, believed to be the oldest ones preserved.

To the Southeast Asian, the creeds related to activities are not to satisfy basic physical needs, but rather for lessening one's emotional burdens. For those tired of struggling for daily bread, these activities help to calm the mind, to cause people to realize they are part of the world as a whole, and to accept that they should lead a worthwhile life in harmony with the universe. Thus, terms like Tea Creed, Flower Creed, Sword Creed, and Kung Fu Creed are frequently heard in Asian cultures. (In terms more familiar to the Westerner, they might be expressed as tea meditation, flower meditation, and so on.) The art of miniature landscapes has actively contributed to the philosophical concept of longevity observed by the Vietnamese. Many Asians regard physical life as short and spiritual life as eternal. To quote Professor Phan Quỳnh again, "One's spirit is part of the universe as a whole."[3]

Hòn Non Bộ at Trấn Quốc Pagoda. The Trấn Quốc Pagoda was built on the Nhị River during the reign of Lý Nam Đế, 544–548 A.D. In 1615, the pagoda was moved because the riverbank had eroded. The age of the Hòn Non Bộ is unknown. Photo by Nguyệt-Mai Đinh.

The Meaning of the Terms

In Vietnamese, four terms are used to denote miniature landscape art: *Giả Sơn, Non Bộ, Núi Non Bộ,* and *Hòn Non Bộ.* The specific definitions are:

Giả Sơn—Giả (Sino-Viet): borrowing, fake, counterfeit, cheat; Sơn (Sino-Viet): mountain. Giả Sơn therefore means a fake mountain, an artificial mountain.[4]

Non Bộ—Non (Nôm): mountain, an abstract term denoting mountainous areas; Bộ (Nôm): shape, silhouette, the way something shows. Non Bộ is a miniature imitation of a real mountain range.[5]

Núi Non Bộ—Similar to Non Bộ; it is a dialect or regional expression. Núi and Non are synonyms meaning mountain.[6]

Hòn Non Bộ at Bến Đục Pagoda, Hà Tây province. The incurved corners are somewhat unusual but are still a traditional form of Hòn Non Bộ containers. Photo by Nguyệt-Mai Đinh.

All three terms, Giả Sơn, Non Bộ, and Núi Non Bộ, mean the same thing, artificial mountain range. Hòn Non Bộ has a different meaning. *Hòn* means island in the ocean, and in Hòn Non Bộ, Hòn symbolizes water. *Non* means mountain; in Hòn Non Bộ, Non symbolizes rock. *Bộ* refers to an entire panorama in which water, mountain, and trees are included. *Bộ* also means to copy the way the scenery (mountains, forest, ocean, animals, birds, structures, and people) looks in miniature. Water, rocks, and trees are the essence of Hòn Non Bộ.

Linguistically, the words *Hòn Non Bộ* are in Nôm, a language of the Mon-Khmer family, known as the oldest language in Southeast Asia.[7] Nôm is a demotic system (meaning it is of or relating to the common people) adapted from the Chinese characters by Vietnamese scholars. As a result, *Hòn* and *Non* and *Bộ* cannot be found in Chinese books, nor are they understood by the Chinese, although the Chinese characters incorporated in Nôm can be.

An approximately 900-year-old Hòn Non Bộ at the temple of Quán Thánh (Saint Mandarin) in Hà Nội. Photo by Nguyệt-Mai Đinh.

Ancient Beliefs

Long ago, the Vietnamese people were called Giao Chỉ, and like many other peoples in Southeast Asia, they worshiped rocks. During the reigns of the first sovereigns of the eighteen kings of Hùng Vương (carbon dating of relics indicates that the first king lived about 4000 years ago), many legendary stories illustrated this custom and tradition. For example, "Trầu Cau" (The Areca Nuts and Betel Plants) tells a story about the close relationships between plants, rocks, and water. Several authors refer to the custom of worshiping stone shapes and trees, especially the hibiscus, *Hibiscus mutabilis* (cotton rose), in many famous novels and short stories. For example, "The Story of Man Nương" (The Lady of Man) tells the story of a woman whose magic power could turn four slabs of rocks into the four goddesses of clouds, rains, thunder, and lightning at the pagoda Dâu; *Lĩnh Nam Chích Quái* (Excerpts of Lĩnh Nam's Extraordinary Story); "The Story of Sơn Tinh Thủy Tinh, Mountain God and Water God" from *Việt Điện U Linh Tập* (Book of Essays on Sacred Brightness); and Truyền Kỳ Mạn Lục (A Collection of Legendary Tales), which is a story about the spirits of a man and a woman who lived in a floss silk tree (*Chorisia speciosa*) in the yard of a Buddhist for over a hundred years.

In *Tang Thương Ngẫu Lục*, the water theme appears again in a tale of the god of the river Dung, whose duty it was to kidnap beautiful girls and force them to be concubines of the Dragon King. *Tang Thương Ngẫu Lục* is not easily translated; Tang Thương is short for Thương Hải Biến Vi Tang Điền, which is an expression denoting the unexpected changes, usually unfavorable, in one's life; Ngẫu Lục refers to a collection of stories related to history, culture, custom, and tradition.

Nam Hải Dị Nhân (Stories About Extraordinary People in Nam Hải) relates that on the mountain of Sóc Sơn there is a huge slab of rock that has a footprint believed to be that of the legendary hero Phù Đổng Thiên Vương, a deity from the heavens who came to help Việt Nam in the struggle against northern invaders. All these stories evidence the concept of rocks having special powers.

Early History of Việt Nam

During the reign of King An Dương Vương (257–207 B.C.), two slabs at the front of the temple of Hùng Vương, called the Slabs of Pledge, were erected as a token of a promise to worship all kings of Hùng Vương, to protect the independence of the country from foreign invaders, and to be devoted to the development of the country.

In the distant past, people from many villages in north Việt Nam put big rocks called Stone Dogs in front of their houses for the purpose of chasing away evil spirits. In reality, most of the rocks did not have the shapes of dogs but were simply powerful looking. King Lê Thánh Tôn, who was noted for being an excellent poet, wrote a poem about a stone dog:

Con Chó Đá

Quyền trọng ơn trên trấn cõi ngoài.
Cửa nghiêm chem chểm một mình ngồi,
Quản bao sương tuyết nào chi kể,
Khéo giữ cao lương cũng chẳng nài.
Mặc khách thị phi giương tráo mắt,
Những lời trần tục biếng vào tai.
Một lòng thờ Chủ, nghìn cân nặng,
Bền vững ai lay cũng chẳng dời.[8]

[The Stone Dog

Power in hand, he sets himself outside.
Alone, he dutifully guards the entrance,
Disregarding what the weather is like,
Nor does he care what is for his meals.
Ins and outs passing by him are all alike,
He puts their words out of his mind,
For his duty is to protect his master
As heavily as his weight; a faithful servant.]

Việt Nam was dominated by northerners almost continuously from 111 B.C. to 938 A.D., with two short periods of independence, first in 40–43 A.D. under the first queen, Trưng Vương, and then in 544–602 A.D. (The period known as "after Lý Nam Đế" began in 548 A.D.) Independence began with the Ngô dynasty in 939 after the liberation of the country. History was again recorded and kept; miniature landscape art was mentioned in books for the first time. There is no record of the art before 939, although it probably did exist.

Later in the tenth century, Đinh Tiên Hoàng won battles against twelve sultans and became king (968–979). He named the Việt Nam of today Đại Cồ Việt, or Great Việt, and established his capital at Hoa Lư, which is now Trường Yên village, Hoa Lư district in Ninh Bình province. If the kings of Hùng Vương were credited with establishing the Vietnamese nation by unifying all other tribes of the Lạc Việt, then King Đinh Tiên Hoàng was responsible for the full independence and the development of the country. From the time of Đinh Tiên Hoàng, the kings in China had to recognize Việt Nam's sovereignty. When he died, his people built a temple in memory of his name.

The temple commemorating King Đinh Tiên Hoàng was designed in the form of "internal: work, external: nation," which means the interior is built in the shape of the Chinese character "kung," 工, meaning work, and the exterior in the shape of the word "kuo," 囯 (the old form of the character), meaning country. The walkway going into the temple has the shape of the word "king," 王. In front of the pavilions Khải Thánh and Nhà Vọng, two gardens are in the shape of the "kuo" character and are full of flowers. In the middle of each garden is a miniature landscape. The one on the left is called Cửu Long Tranh Châu (Nine Dragons Fight for a Pearl); the one on the right is Hình Nhân Bái Tướng (An Old Fisherman Prays for Good Weather).[9] The landscape on the right reflects the wish made not only by fishermen but by all

Hòn Non Bộ (Dancing Phoenix) in Ninh Bình province was built during the reign of King Lê Đại Hành. Photo by Nguyệt-Mai Đinh.

peasants for moderate weather with sufficient water for their rice and other crops. That landscape is in a square shallow container.

When King Đinh Tiên Hoàng was assassinated, his son was too young for national affairs, and this allowed the seventh king of the Song dynasty of China to launch an invasion. The queen, the young king's mother, and the regent Phạm Cự Lượng urged Lê Hoàn, then the commanding general of the army, to take over the throne with the title Lê Đại Hành (980–1005), establishing the Pre- Lê dynasty. The capital sat at Hoa Lư as before.

According to *Việt Sử Lược* (A Summary of Việt History)—the second history written in the fourteenth century; the first had been destroyed—in 984, the Year of the Monkey and the fourth year of the reign of his royal eminence, Thiên Phúc (meaning Lucky Forever; his name was Lê Đại Hành, and he assumed a new appellation upon ascending to the throne, a common practice for early Vietnamese

Hòn Non Bộ inside the Temple of Literacy Shrine, part of Việt Nam's first university located in what is now Hà Nội. The openings in the stones are reminiscent of the caves the ancients believed were the homes of the gods. Photo by Nguyệt-Mai Đinh.

rulers), the king built seven palaces with pillars that were covered with gold and silver (the roof tiles of one were covered with silver). He also built a two-level building, and surrounded it and the seven palaces with gardens. They were the Bạch Bảo, Phong Lưu, Vinh Hoa, Bồng Lai, Cực Lạc, Hỏa Vân, Trường Xuân, and Long Lộc palaces.[10]

The material used to create artificial mountains was bamboo, and the composition was called Giả Sơn. Lê Đại Hành had one built called Nam Sơn (South Mountain), a phrase people use to wish others longevity. It is not certain when people began using rocks and placing them in a container called Bể Cạn (shallow container), adding plants, and calling the composition Hòn Non Bộ, but it is believed the first may have been at Lê Đại Hành's palaces.

During the next dynasty—the Lý dynasty—the people of Trường Yên constructed two temples to commemorate the merits of the Kings Đinh Tiên Hoàng and Lê Đại Hành. Weather-beaten over time, the two temples deteriorated. In the seventeenth century, Bùi Thời Trung, a high-ranking mandarin in the royal court had the temples rebuilt so that their previously north-facing facades were turned to the east. In 1676, the temples underwent major maintenance, and the last major repair was done in 1898 in the reign of King Thành Thái. The floors were elevated and the thresholds were made of rocks we can still see today.

When Lít Phan went to Ninh Binh province in northern Việt Nam to visit these two temples where the kings are commemorated, he saw that in front of the temples there are five Hòn Non Bộ made of rocks. Each of the miniature landscapes is in the middle of a shallow container. No extra features like statuettes or human figures were added; there were only rocks and plants.

In front of the temple commemorating King Lê Đại Hành (of the first Lê dynasty) is a Hòn Non Bộ of solid granite that is carved in the shape of a dancing phoenix, and that, if viewed from the north side, resembles the queen. Viewed from the southwest side, it looks like a lion. At the bottom of the miniature mountain are four noble animals: a dragon, a heavenly dog, a turtle, and a phoenix. The little mountain is placed in the middle of a hexagonal shallow container, and on the mountain there is a *Ficus retusa*. This Hòn Non Bộ composition serves the purpose of *feng shui* because it is positioned symbolically to block the right passage leading to a sacred room.

To the left of the temple is a pond where the king passed his time enjoying the lotus and fish. On each side of the Ritual Room, which is further back in the temple, there are two pavilions where elders in the area would meet to discuss the festivals or celebrations to be held. In front of these two pavilions are two Hòn Non Bộ; one looks like a phoenix hatching her eggs, and the other like a phoenix dancing.

Ngô Sĩ Liên's *Đại Việt Sử Ký Toàn Thư* (Encyclopedic Book of Great Nam History) has these lines: "In the Year of the Monkey, the fifth year of the reign of Thiên Phúc, in spring, February of the lunar year, copper was minted into sovereigns; buildings and houses with gold gilt pillars were built in Đại Vân mountain."[11] Architecture in the Lê dynasty, especially in the reign of King Lê Đại Hành, developed fully. This period marked the stable independence of the country, and the people enjoyed both new trends from the south and influences from China.

The Later Lý Dynasty (1009–1225)

A devoted bonze named Vạn Hạnh and a chancellor named Đào Cam Mộc both supported the crowning of Lý Công Uẩn, commanding general of the royal garrison, as the first king of the later Lý dynasty, titled Lý Thái Tổ. The king had the capital moved from Hoa Lư to Đại La (the former name for Hà Nội), which he renamed Thăng Long following a dream he had when his royal boat was anchored at the new capital.

It is recorded in history books that King Lý used bamboo to make artificial mountains. The book *Việt Sử Lược* (A Summary of Viet History) states:

> In June of the lunar year, the birthday month of the king called Thiên Thánh, "Heavenly Saint" (1028), the construction of Eternity Mountains at Long Trì was completed. The range has five mountains, four in the four corners and one in the middle. On the top of the middle one, there is a picture denoting longevity, accompanied by many white herons. Above the mountains hang many figures of fairies and birds in flight. The mountains are full of animals and dragons. Flags and pennants are on posts, gold pieces and other jewels are hanging. Many groups of children in chorus entertain at the ceremony.[12]

A second book, *Khâm Định Việt Sử Thông Giám Cương Mục* (Text and Explanation Making a Complete Mirror for the Vietnamese History Established by Imperial Orders), explains in detail:

> To celebrate his birthday, he had bamboo made into mountains which were called Eternity of South Mountains, including five mountains, in the middle of which is the mountain called Eternity Mountain; four others are White Herons decorated with white birds, animals, flags and pennants. The art of building artificial mountains has flourished since then.[13]

Việt Sử Lược states about a later king:

In the Year of the Cat, the third year of the reign of the king who chose the royal title Sùng Hưng Đại Bảo (1051), two ponds, called Thụy Thanh and Ứng Minh, were dug in the royal garden Thắng Cảnh. In the Year of the Pig (1203), King Lý Cao Tông had more buildings and pavilions built: the Phú Quốc, Phương Tiêu, and Thấu Viên, with a fishpond that was connected to a river. On the bank of this pond was a summerhouse with many different kinds of flowers. The house was built with carved pillars and rafts, one of the most magnificent structures of the time.[14]

Miniature landscapes were created as Hòn Non Bộ, but they were also memorialized in other ways. In his book *L'Art du Vietnam* (The Art of Việt Nam), Josef Hejzlar includes many photographs of miniature landscapes carved on wood that

Hòn Non Bộ at Ngọc Sơn Temple, Hà Nội. Rarely, if ever, is a temple found without an accompanying Hòn Non Bộ. Photo by Nguyệt-Mai Đinh.

are believed to have existed since the Lý dynasty. According to Hejzlar, they are preserved at Ninh Phúc pagoda, north of Bút Tháp hamlet, Nhạn Tháp village, Thuận Thành district, Bắc Ninh province.[15] The carvings show trees, rocks, and water, the same objects of worship that led to the creation of Hòn Non Bộ.

During the Lý dynasty, Ma Văn Cao wrote a series of novels titled *Lĩnh Nam Dật Sử* (The Missing History of the Southeast), written in Mon, with an introduction by General Trần Nhật Duật of the Trần dynasty. The series was translated into Sino in 1297 and into present-day Vietnamese by Bùi Đàm. Ma Văn Cao wrote about a young girl named Quý Nhi, who married into a noble family and for the first time in her life saw what the garden of a rich family looked like.

> Quý Nhi, Precious Child, enters the garden, where she sees a mountain, at the foot of which is a small palace surrounded with all kinds of amazing flowers. On the right side of the palace is a Hòn Non Bộ; there is a glint to it from precious stone. Under it a stream runs to a pond, whose water is very serene with its surface like a mirror. Next to the Hòn Non Bộ is a winding path for strollers with nerium [oleander] on both sides.[16]

The Trần Dynasty (1225–1400)

King Lý Huệ Tông did not have any sons, so he had to pass the throne to his daughter, Princess Chiêu Thánh, who was crowned as Lý Chiêu Hoàng. The queen's regent was Trần Thủ Độ, an expedient man who forced her to give up the throne to her husband, Trần Cảnh, the regent's relative, thus establishing the Trần dynasty. The Trần family ruled the country for 174 years. The capital was at Thăng Long. Many buildings and pavilions were constructed during the Trần dynasty, adding to those built during the Lý dynasty.

Ngô Sĩ Liên says in his *Encyclopedic Book of Great Nam History*:

> In the reign of King Trần Thái Tông (1230), many structures, such as Thái Tử palace, Quang Triều palace, and two big houses in the east and the west of the royal citadel, were constructed. In 1248, Lâm Ba bridge from Chân Giáo pagoda to Ngoại Thiềm lake and Thái Thanh palace was built. In each palace, as well as each house, there were miniature landscapes as decoration.[17]

In *Mỹ Thuật Cổ Truyền Việt Nam* (Traditional Arts of Việt Nam), Nguyễn Khắc Ngữ offers accounts of pillars made of wood, on which fairies with human heads and bird bodies were holding pots of flowers in their hands. They were also on the stands for gongs at Thái Lạc, Văn Lâm, Hưng Yên pagodas, and at Hang pagoda in Hoàng Liên Sơn province.[18]

During the Trần Dynasty, Confucianism, Taoism, and Buddhism were developing. National examinations for governmental positions were organized regularly. Both Sino and Nôm orthographs became very popular. Unfortunately, after three invasions by the Yuan in the north, most of the magnificent palaces in Thăng Long were completely destroyed. When the wars were over, the king had the palaces and buildings rebuilt, using as the labor force people who had collaborated with the enemy. He also had many Hòn Non Bộ built right in the middle of small lakes, with marine plants and creatures like fish and turtles. Around the lakes, trees such as spruce and cypress and rare flowers were grown.

By the end of the reign of the Trần dynasty, around 1363, Trần Dụ Tông had a big lake dug in back of his palace and had rocks piled up in the shape of a mountain, around which many kinds of trees and flowers were planted. Cages for rare birds

One of the larger Hòn Non Bộ in front of Hòn Non Nước pagoda containing water lilies and other plants. Photo by Nguyệt-Mai Đinh.

and rare wild animals were installed around this artificial mountain. On the shore he had two big cinnamon trees planted. A building was constructed nearby, called Song Quế (Twin Cinnamon) and later renamed Lạc Thanh (Sound of Joy). In addition, there were many other smaller lakes containing salt water for sea creatures like green turtles and fish, special lakes for crocodiles, as well as a lake for carp.

The Hồ and Lê Lợi's Uprising (1401–1427)

In 1400, Hồ Quý Ly dethroned Đế and crowned himself king. A year later, he resigned to become Thái Thượng Hoàng, "Extremely Great Emperor," a term inherited from the Lý dynasty as the king resigned and ceded the throne to his selected son.

On 21 August 1406, the Ming king of China ordered Chu Năng, one of his generals, to command an army to invade Việt Nam, confiscate all things related to Vietnamese culture, such as books and artworks, and bring them back to China. In 1407,

Hòn Non Bộ in back garden of pagoda, Central Việt Nam. The carved stone pieces are grave markers. Photo by Nguyệt-Mai Đinh.

Hồ Quý Ly was caught by the invaders. In the carnage that followed, all works of art and architecture were destroyed. Hòn Non Bộ suffered the same fate as the other arts.

In the Year of the Dog (1418), Lê Lợi, supported by Nguyễn Trãi, an excellent strategist and military genius, revolted against the Ming conquerors. In ten arduous years, he completely wiped out the invaders and crowned himself Thái Tử, the first king of the Post-Lê dynasty. He seated his capital at Thăng Long, which he renamed Đông Đô (Eastern Capital), and renamed the country Đại Việt (Great Việt).

After fighting with the Chinese from 1424 to 1427, Lê Thái Tổ became king. During the Lê dynasty (1428–1527), he and his successors had all palaces, buildings, and artwork restored. Two of these were in Đông Kinh (now Hà Nội) and Lam Kinh (now Thanh Hóa). In Đông Kinh, the king had a grand garden, called the Royal Elevated Garden, with deer and impala and numerous rare animals; historians remarked that it was greater and more beautiful than ever before. In Lam Kinh, the native village of the King, which is in Lam Sơn in Thanh Hóa province, many palaces were constructed in places where the conquering army had devastated all that had been there before. Most of the members of the Lê royal family were buried there. The architectural style was similar to that of summerhouses, with flowerbeds surrounding every structure. Hòn Non Bộ was the king's favorite, and it was used to enhance the scene with special features.

The miniscenes and miniature landscapes made during this period used *Cycas revoluta* (sago palms) on the birthdays of the kings, lords, and elderly high-class people. In addition, plants and miniature landscapes were forms of decoration in places of worship and temples, and provided elegant entertainment for people of all walks of life.

The Mạc Dynasty (1527–1592)

In 1527, General Mạc Đăng Dung usurped the powers of King Lê and became King Mạc Đăng Dung. During the Mạc Đăng Dung dynasty, many imperial palaces with beautiful landscapes, including those with Hòn Non Bộ, were built. The area where the palaces were built was called Dương Kinh, meaning the Capital of Dương, in Hải Dương province.

When King Mạc Đăng Dung assumed the throne, General Nguyễn Kim relocated to Laos to support Lê Trang Tông, who became a king in Laos in 1532 before moving back to South Việt Nam and creating a southern dynasty there. In 1545, General Nguyễn Kim died of poisoning and his son-in-law Trịnh Kiểm took over the position of general. Together with King Lê Trang Tông, Trịnh Kiểm returned to Thanh Hóa in north Việt Nam. At the time, the country of Việt Nam did not extend very far south; nevertheless, the two kingdoms were referred to as the north dynasty, which was governed by King Mạc Đăng Doanh, and the south dynasty, which was governed by King Lê Trang Tông. Thus, Việt Nam had two dynasties, the Mạc and the Lê dynasties, both of which continued until 1788 when Nguyễn Huệ became the northern king and his older brother, Nguyễn Nhạc, became the southern king. Not until 1802 did Nguyễn Ánh unify the country.

Hòn Non Bộ has, to some extent, been used in predicting one's fate or destiny. A story found in many Vietnamese history books is about a scholar named Trạng Trình (1491–1585) who used Hòn Non Bộ to provide guidance. The story goes:

> When Việt Nam was in the reign of what was called "King Lê and Lord Trịnh," Nguyễn Hoàng, a brother-in-law of Lord Trịnh Kiểm, was among those Trịnh Kiểm wanted to get rid of because the lord was afraid that some day Nguyễn would overthrow him in the north. To get away from trouble, Nguyễn Hoàng asked the lord to be assigned governor at Thuận Hoá. He secretly sent someone to seek advice from Trạng Trình, a scholar of the time, who was living at Hải Dương province. Without answering the messenger directly, the scholar walked with his cane to a Hòn Non Bộ, at the foot of which a colony of ants was busily working. Looking at the Hòn Non Bộ [which was a long, low horizontal mountain], he said: "Hoành Sơn Nhất Đái Vạn Đại Dung Thân," meaning "Go to the other side of the mountain range and stay there in safety forever." Obediently, Nguyễn Hoàng asked his sister Ngọc Bảo, Trịnh Kiểm's wife, for help. Nguyễn Hoàng's wish was granted.[19]

Many years later, Nguyễn Ánh, Nguyễn Hoàng's descendant, unified the country and became the first king of the Nguyễn dynasty in 1802.

Hòn Non Bộ wove through the fabric of Vietnamese life in all dynasties. One example is in *Vũ Trung Tuỳ Bút* (Encyclopedic Anthology) by Phạm Đình Hổ (1768–1829), which was written in Sino and translated by Đông Châu:

> In the years of the Horse and the Goat (1774–1775), people everywhere were enjoying peace and prosperity. Lord Trịnh Sâm (1767–1782) took some time to visit here and there because he loved landscapes. He frequently came to Tây Hồ (West Lake), near the Tử Trầm mountain, or to Dũng Thuý mountain, where he had many structures built.

In every corner of the buildings or structures in the palace, he had Hòn Non Bộ created. In addition, he had many kinds of birds, animals, plants, and flowers collected to put in these structures, making them magnificent places for visitors. During the night, these birds and animals made noises that could be heard from a far distance. Many scholars and intellectuals of the time believed that was an unusual omen.[20]

In 1782, Lord Trịnh Sâm summoned Hải Thượng Lãng Ông (1724–1791), a famous medical man of Việt Nam, to Thăng Long to cure the lord's child. After the visit, the medical man described, in his memoir about the capital, what he saw at the Tử Các (Red Pavilion): "Walking for some time, one comes to a checkpoint where a unit of the royal garrison was posted. The checkpoint was situated by a big lake, around which one could see many rare and strange kinds of flowers and Hòn Non Bộ—very unusual to the eyes."[21]

Hòn Non Bộ, as well as miniature plants and rocks, are mentioned in *Đoạn Trường Tân Thanh* (The Story of Kiều), a thousand-page book by Nguyễn Du

Hòn Non Bộ in front of the Nha Trang Oceanography Institute, Central Việt Nam. Modern buildings continue the custom of making a Hòn Non Bộ a part of their landscape. Photo by Nguyệt-Mai Đinh.

(1765–1820). Three quotations are given here, not to prove that Hòn Non Bộ existed during the period but rather to show that the art form was enjoyed widely by all classes of people.

The first quotation tells of the time when Kim Trọng studied at Ngôi Việt, a merchant's residence right behind Thuý Kiều's house:

> Lấy điều du học hỏi thuê,
> Túi đàn, cặp sách, để huề dọn sang.
> Có cây, có đá sẵn sàng,
> Có hiên Lãm Thuý, nét vàng chưa phai.[22]

[That he is a foreign student looking for lodging
Is clear: instrument bag and book box are evident.
The tree, the rocks are there
He came here to study
Under the shade of unfaded vestibule.]

The second reference describes Thuý Kiều coming from her house to Kim Trọng's:

> Lần theo núi giả đi vòng,
> Cuối tường dường có nẻo thông mới rào.
> Xắn tay mở khoá động đào
> Rẽ mây trong tỉ lối vào thiên-thai.[23]

[Circumventing along the artificial mountain,
To the newly made gate at the wall's end,
(She) raised her hand to open it,
And stepped into the land of bliss.]

The third occurs at a small temple, where Thuý Kiều, under Hoạn Thư's instruction, led a secluded life by taking care of the temple and saying prayers daily.

> Sẵn Quan Âm các vườn ta,
> Có cây trăm thước, có hoa bốn mùa.
> Có cổ thụ, có sơn hồ,
> Cho nàng ra đó giữ chùa tụng kinh.[24]

[Quan Âm's statue is in the garden,
With trees a hundred feet tall and flowers all year round.
With old trees, a lake, and a mountain.
Let her (Thuý Kiều) stay there for prayers.]

The Tây Sơn (1789–1801)

The king of Việt Nam in the latter part of the eighteenth century, Lê Chiêu Thống, was not widely supported. Taking advantage of the political decline in Việt Nam during this period, Càn Long, the Manchurian emperor in China, had Tôn Sĩ Nghị command 200,000 men to invade Việt Nam. They occupied Thăng Long.

Nguyễn Huệ, a hero from Tây Sơn village, Qui Nhơn district in Bình Định province, together with his brothers Nguyễn Nhạc and Nguyễn Lữ, rose up against the invaders. Huệ laid claim to the title Bắc Bình Vương, "Northern Pacifying King." On 25 November in the Year of the Monkey (1788), Huệ crowned himself emperor, bestowing on himself the royal title Quang Trung, and he commanded his army to the north. Within seven days, he completely defeated the 200,000 Manchurian troops, forcing Tôn Sĩ Nghị to flee home. The battle ended on 5 January in the Year of the Rooster (1789).

Having won the war, Quang Trung returned to Phú Xuân (present-day Huế), where he died in 1792. His ten-year-old son succeeded with the royal title Cảnh Thịnh. Due to the new king's youth, the mandarins in the court became fractious, and the instability allowed Nguyễn Ánh, a descendent of Lord Nguyễn's family, to seek revenge and return the family to power. When Nguyễn Ánh became king, he had all remainders of the Tây Sơn works and art destroyed. Consequently, no books or materials related to Hòn Non Bộ during this period can be found.

The Nguyễn Dynasty (1802–1945)

Vietnamese Art and Architecture

During the reign of the Nguyễn dynasty, Vietnamese arts and architecture were influenced by the French and Chinese. Assisted by Pierre Joseph Georges Pigneau de Béhaine, French legions, and the armies of Thailand and Cambodia, Nguyễn Ánh defeated Tây Sơn, and became the first king of the Nguyễn dynasty with the royal title Gia Long. He established the capital at Phú Xuân (now Huế). Throughout this period of French influence, Hòn Non Bộ, like much else of Vietnamese culture, continued essentially unchanged. Although the French became more and more dominant, they made no attempt to change the Vietnamese culture. Their interests lay in dominating the politics and economics of the country, not the art, history, or culture.

French Influence

In his struggle against the Tây Sơn, Nguyễn Ánh had asked Pierre Joseph Georges Pigneau de Béhaine to recruit manpower and raise funds for weapons. As a result, the French presence in Việt Nam played an important role in developing architecture. According to Nguyễn Khắc Ngữ's *Mỹ Thuật Cổ Truyền Việt Nam* (Traditional Arts of Việt Nam), French officers helped Nguyễn Ánh build the Huế Royal Citadel, the Phiên An and Hà Nội citadels, and many other small fortified posts throughout the country. Nguyễn Khắc Ngữ writes, "the architectural style is similar to that of Vauban in France."[25]

Chinese Influence

Most royal tombs of the kings of the Nguyễn dynasty contain a garden with beautifully arranged plants and flowers around a lake, exactly like those of the Manchurian kings of the Qing dynasty. The capital, the Forbidden Citadel, where the king and his family lived and worked, also contained a royal garden:

> The summerhouse Trường Du, built in 1849, is located in the eastern part of the garden, looking out on a very deep rectangular lake. In front of the house, under a temple, a bridge extends across the south side of the lake.

Hòn Non Bộ in front of the Den of the Kings of the Nguyễn dynasty, Huế province, Central Việt Nam. In general, the larger and more important the edifice, the larger and more important the Hòn Non Bộ. Photo by Nguyệt-Mai Đinh.

On the left and right sides of the lake there are two huge Hòn Non Bộ, to which five small temples were added. A small bridge connects these two Hòn Non Bộ.[26]

Another huge Hòn Non Bộ can be found in front of Thái Bình Lâu (Extreme Peace Pavilion), in Thiên Phương Garden, where the king passed his time reading books. The artificial mountain was built in the middle of a deep, rectangular lake and is accessible by three bridges. This Hòn Non Bộ is very much like the one in Suzhou, China, called Sơn Thủy Bồn Cảnh (Landscape in the Water Tank) because the road leading to the artificial mountain is paved with cobblestone and because many big trees grow higher than the mountain, making the whole structure unbalanced.

Along with the art of miniature landscape, the art of miniature plants, called Cây Kiểng (similar to Japanese bonsai), flourished during the Nguyễn dynasty. Many different classes of people participated in the art of Cây Kiểng: the kings enjoyed planting pines and junipers; the mandarins loved growing *Thuja orientalis* (arborvitae) and *Casuarina* (beefwood); intellectuals or other notable figures liked figs, such as *Ficus benjamina, F. elastica, F. religiosa,* and *F. retusa;* and lay people devoted themselves to planting mallow, *Tamarindus indica* (tamarind), and *Melaleuca leucadendra* (cajeput). Except for those planted by the kings, all trees planted for pleasure by the mandarins or lay people had to have their tops bent downward because it was considered impertinent to superiors to have the treetops grow upward.

The term used for these miniature plants used to be *cây cảnh,* meaning plants in pots; in the south, it is *cây kiểng.* The word *cảnh* had to be pronounced slightly differently to avoid sounding like the name of a high-ranking mandarin, Nguyễn Hữu Cảnh, the general governor of lowland Cambodia. It is said that Nguyễn Hữu Cảnh himself had to change his name from Cảnh to Kính to differentiate it from the name of Prince Cảnh, King Gia Long's son.

By the time that the Nguyễn dynasty ended, the arts of miniature landscapes and miniature plants had become a favored pastime of the people in Việt Nam. There are Hòn Non Bộ accompanied by miniature plants in temples, offices, and pagodas, in the city as well as in the countryside, and in front of houses. They serve dual purposes: enhancing the beauty of the houses and freeing people's minds from stress and worry.

> Making a modern-day Hòn Non Bộ builds on and continues a long tradition of belief in the power of rocks and an appreciation of the beauty of mountains and plants.

Notes

Note that publishing companies are not always given in Vietnamese references. Year of publication may not be given either, especially for Vietnamese books republished in the United States.

1. Phan Quỳnh, "Non Bộ Trong Lịch Sử Việt Nam" (Non Bộ in the History of Việt Nam), *Người Việt* (Daily News), Westminster, California, 11 May 1996, No. 3808; based on Nguyễn Đăng Thục, *Lịch Sử Tư Tưởng Việt Nam* (The History of Vietnamese Ideologies), Nhà Xuất Bản Thành phố Hồ Chí Minh, Hồ Chí Minh City, Việt Nam, reprinted 1998, volume 1, pp. 87–108, 114.

2. Phan Quỳnh, "Philosophy of Non Bộ," speech to Hòn Non Bộ Association, Balboa Park, San Diego, California, 6 August 1995.

3. Phan Quỳnh, "Philosophy of Non Bộ," speech to Hòn Non Bộ Association, Balboa Park, San Diego, California, 6 August 1995.

4. Trần Trọng San and Trần Trọng Tuyên, *Hán Việt Tự Điển* (Sino-Vietnamese Dictionary), no publisher, Scarborough, Ontario, Canada, 1997, p. 25 and p. 133.

5. Huỳnh Tịnh Paulus Của, *Đại Nam Quốc Âm Tự Vị* (Dictionary of Great Nam National Phonology), Văn Hữu, Gia Định, Việt Nam, 1974, p. 62 and p. 158.

6. Huỳnh Tịnh Paulus Của, *Đại Nam Quốc Âm Tự Vị* (Dictionary of Great Nam National Phonology), Văn Hữu, Gia Định, Việt Nam, 1974, p. 62, p. 158, and p.163.

Hòn Non Bộ inside a train station office in Sài Gòn. It is located in a central position so that all passersby can enjoy it. Photo by Nguyệt-Mai Đinh.

7. Anthony Trần Văn Kiệm, *Giúp Đọc Nôm và Hán Việt* (Handbook on How to Read Demotic Nôm and Sino-Vietnamese Terms).

8. Dương Quảng Hàm, *Việt Nam Thi Văn Hợp Tuyển* (Selected Vietnamese Poetry and Literature), Xuân Thu, Los Alamitos, California, n.d., p. 52.

9. Nguyễn Văn Trò và Dương Thanh Lam, *Di Tích và Thắng Cảnh Hoa Lư* (History of Hoa Lư Landscapes and Historical Landmarks), Phòng Văn Thể Huyện Hoa Lư (Office of Cultural and Sport Activity in Hoa Lư), Việt Nam, 1997, pp. 13–14.

10. No author, *Việt Sử Lược* (A Summary of Viet History), translated by Trần Quốc Vượng, Văn Sử Địa, Hà Nội, Việt Nam, 1960, p. 57.

11. Ngô Sĩ Liên, *Đai Việt Sử Ký Toàn Thư* (Encyclopedic Book of Great Nam History), volume 1, Khoa Học Xã Hội, Hà Nội, Việt Nam, 1993, pp. 222–223.

12. No author, *Việt Sử Lược* (A Summary of Viet History), translated by Trần Quốc Vượng, Văn Sử Địa, Hà Nội, Việt Nam, 1960, p. 78.

13. Multiple authors, *Khâm Định Việt Sử Thông Giám Cương Mục* (Text and Explanation Making a Complete Mirror for the Vietnamese History Established by Imperial Orders), quoted in "Việt Time," volume 3, issue 36, 15 July 1993, p. 58.

14. No author, *Việt Sử Lược* (A Summary of Viet History), translated by Trần Quốc Vượng, Văn Sử Địa, Hà Nội, Việt Nam, 1960, pp. 91 and 166.

15. Josef Hejzlar, W. and B. Forman, *L'Art du Vietnam* (The Art of Việt Nam), Paris, 1973, quoted in "Việt Time," volume 3, issue 36, 15 July 1993, p. 58.

16. Bùi Đàm, *Lĩnh Nam Dật Sử* (The Missing History of the Southeast), quoted in "Việt Time," volume 3, issue 36, 15 July 1993, p. 58.

17. Ngô Sĩ Liên, *Đai Việt Sử Ký Toàn Thư* (Encyclopedic Book of Great Nam History), volume 2, Khoa Học Xã Hội, Hà Nội, Việt Nam, 1993, pp. 12 and 21.

18. Nguyễn Khắc Ngữ, *Mỹ Thuật Cổ Truyền Việt Nam* (Traditional Arts of Việt Nam), Làng Văn Publishing Co., Montreal, 1981, p. 93.

19. Trần Trọng Kim, *Việt Nam Sử Lược* (History of Việt Nam), volume 2, Đại Nam, Glendale, California, 1976, p. 30.

20. Dương Quảng Hàm, *Việt Nam Văn Học Sử Yếu* (A Concise Book of Vietnamese Literature), Sài Gòn [publisher], Sài Gòn [location], Việt Nam, 1958, pp. 116–117. Republished in Nam Phong "South Wind" magazine, volume 21, edition 121.

21. Dương Quảng Hàm, *Việt Nam Văn Học Sử Yếu* (A Concise Book of Vietnamese Literature), Sài Gòn [publisher], Sài Gòn [location], Việt Nam, 1958, p. 300.

22. Nguyễn Du, *Truyện Thúy Kiều: Đoạn Trường Tân Thanh* (The Tale of Thúy Kiều's Broken Heart), revised by Bùi Kỷ Và Trần Trọng Kim, Đại Nam, Glendale, California, 1995, p. 72.

23. Nguyễn Du, *Truyện Thúy Kiều: Đoạn Trường Tân Thanh* (The Tale of Thúy Kiều's Broken Heart), revised by Bùi Kỷ Và Trần Trọng Kim, Đại Nam, Glendale, California, 1995, p. 78.

24. Nguyễn Du, *Truyện Thúy Kiều: Đoạn Trường Tân Thanh* (The Tale of Thúy Kiều's Broken Heart), revised by Bùi Kỷ Và Trần Trọng Kim, Đại Nam, Glendale, California, 1995, p. 153.

25. Nguyễn Khắc Ngữ, *Mỹ Thuật Cổ Truyền Việt Nam* (Traditional Arts of Việt Nam), Làng Văn Publishing Co., Montreal, 1981, p. 291.

26. Phan Thuận An, Tôn Thất Bình, Lê Hoa Chi, Việt Dũng, Anh Sơn, Thanh Tùng, and Duy Từ, *Cố Đô Huế Đẹp Và Thơ* (The Ancient Capital of Huế, Poetic and Beautiful), Thuận Hóa, Quảng Trị, Việt Nam, 1992, p. 73.

Mẫu Tử Tình Thâm (Mother and Son)

Enjoying the Art of Miniature Landscapes

Imagine slipping through the little passes and valleys of the mini-mountains, floating on the tiny streams of water, or resting in the shade of a tree by the side of a bridge leading into a cavern.

Themes of Miniature Landscape Art

The main themes of miniature landscape art are mountains and islands with some plants, all of which are placed in a shallow basin similar to a tray made of clay. Traditionally, the Hòn Non Bộ was placed in the middle of a rectangular water container made of bricks and stucco. It was arranged in such a way that it looked like an island amidst a body of water, especially the sea. Now many Hòn Non Bộ are in shallow, tray-like containers, convenient for indoor or outdoor decoration.

To some extent, this art has been an indicator of social status and wealth. By looking at the composition, one could tell what type of people its owners were and whether they were rich or poor. In the old days, the trees grown on a miniature artificial mountain would reveal whether its owners were members of the royal family (who would grow pines and junipers), high-ranking mandarins (who would grow *Thuja orientalis* and *Casuarina*), intellectuals (*Ficus* of various kinds), or lay people (tamarind and melaleuca).[1] Since the late eighteenth century, however, these indicators have not been so strictly observed. As a result, anyone from any class—depending on personal taste—can enjoy growing any kind of tree.

Viewing Hòn Non Bộ is an out-of-this-world experience; the viewer becomes part of the scene. Imagine that under a trellis of climbing flowers, there is a Hòn

Non Bộ with a basin in which goldfish swim playfully. Halfway up a mountain covered with mosses and a few trees there is a small pagoda with steps and a bridge over a stream. Somewhere on the mountain there is a big, old tree (for instance, a banyan), under whose shade two elderly men play checkers. At the foot of the mountain, by the stream, there are four figures representing the humble way of life in the countryside: a fisherman, a woodcutter, a peasant plowing his field, and a scholar reading a book. It is as if a beautiful area in the real world were reduced to scale, yet with the caverns, the streams, and the worn path up the mountain appearing as large as life.[2]

Miniature Landscapes

Some Hòn Non Bộ are rather big, as much as 20 to 25 feet (6 to 7.5 m) high or more. Most, however, are smaller. If possible, the mountain in a Hòn Non Bộ is one solid piece of rock with the form of a real mountain. If not, fragments of rocks of different shapes and sizes are pieced together to make tiny mountains. Piecing the rocks together is a wise idea if the Hòn Non Bộ is to be moved or taken to a show and put on display.

The mountain may be built in a large basin in a corner of the garden or in a lotus lake in front of the summerhouse. Those who do not have spacious areas may enjoy the art by reducing the whole scene to an even smaller scale, as small as a tea tray, to be put on an end table or on a low shelf.

The Hòn Non Bộ shown in the photographs that appear in this chapter was built in a corner of a garden, based on a dream of the wife in the household. (Minh Trần and his wife, Hòa Trần, gave permission to use their names in this book and very kindly allowed us to take pictures at their home.) Quan Âm, a female Buddha, appeared to the wife in a dream and said the house would prosper if a Hòn Non Bộ were placed in a specific corner of the garden with a dragon in it for luck. Later she attended a show of Hòn Non Bộ in Balboa Park in San Diego, where she met Lít Phan. He agreed to build the Hòn Non Bộ, although he had not done garden Hòn Non Bộ before.

Because of the long intertwining of the Vietnamese and Chinese cultures (albeit unwilling on the part of the Vietnamese), many customs and beliefs found in China are also present in Việt Nam. *Feng shui* is one of these. *Feng* (wind) *shui* (water) can roughly be described as a system with rules for creating a comfortable, pleasant, positive environment using light, objects, colors, and direction and position. Some Westerners accomplish this by hiring architects and interior decorators in whom they believe; some Asians accomplish this through their beliefs in the rules of *feng shui.*

If a Hòn Non Bộ were built in the front yard, according to the principles of *feng shui* the mountain could not be placed directly in front of the door, but rather would have to be to the left side as one looks out from the house. The pond holding the Hòn Non Bộ could extend directly in front of the house. In any case, the walk from the street to the door would have had to curve around the right side of the Hòn Non Bộ rather than coming directly from the street to the door.

The dragon theme appears frequently in Asian art and culture. While Europeans and Americans consider dragons to be fierce, frightening creatures, and ancient cartographers used dragons and sea serpents to show dangerous, uncharted waters, Asians believe dragons to be friendly, lucky, positive, and benevolent. Asian legend has it that a dragon used its feet and tail to create rivers and streams, so

Garden Hòn Non Bộ by Lít Phan. Since the plants have unlimited root space, they will need more trimming than those in pots.

The main mountain of Lít Phan's Garden Hòn Non Bộ. One mountain must be taller than all the rest to show its importance.

Quan Âm, a favorite woman Buddha who
has great status among those who have
achieved Buddhahood, on the mountaintop
of Lít Phan's Garden Hòn Non Bộ.

Dragon in Garden Hòn Non Bộ. The waterfall
in this garden becomes a small stream that
feeds a pond. The sides of the stream are
lined with a series of rocks that gives the impression of a dragon looking over his shoulder.

draining the land after a great flood and allowing people to return to their homes and their earlier way of life.

Shallow Containers and Hòn Non Bộ

Much of the enjoyment of Hòn Non Bộ comes from the pleasure of seeing real water and the reflection of the mountains in it. It is important to explain why the water container used for Hòn Non Bộ is a shallow container. Hòn Non Bộ is a reduced form of an actual scene in nature, often that of an island standing alone in an area of the sea close to the shore. The open sea is symbolized by the water in the container in which a Hòn Non Bộ is built. It is only necessary to have the surface of the water; depth is not important. One does not ordinarily look deep into the ocean, but merely at the waves on the surface. In the days before cement was available as a building material, lime mixed with other substances was used as stucco to build these containers. Later, when cement was available and construction became easier, the containers were made deeper with glass in the walls in places, and more fish were added to the tank. The viewer could see the weeds, the reef, and the remains of wrecked ships.[3]

Enjoying the Art

Enjoying miniature landscape art is a form of meditation. People have to struggle in their lives every day for survival or to reach their goals of security and a good reputation. This art brings to their minds calmness, self-control, and emptiness (emptiness is a meditative state of mind in which the mind ceases to be active with thoughts and is accompanied by a deep physical relaxation), which is very useful for relieving stress. The more they are engaged in this art, the more they can keep themselves from being distracted by worldly desires.

Gazing at a Hòn Non Bộ, viewers will surely let their minds join the scene in silence and tranquility. Everything is the same, but one thing has changed: their view. Each item in the miniature landscape provides some inspiration or serves as a reminder. Looking at a bonze meditating in the cavern of the mini-mountain, viewers will associate themselves with the meditator and, in a moment, may be convinced that practicing religion is the only way to keep from being caught up in the chaos and troubles of life. Looking at two mystical figures playing checkers, the viewers see them always there, whereas the moves on the checkerboard of life occur swiftly. The viewer realizes the impermanence of everything.

Detail of Hòn Non Bộ (Stone Bridge). The water carrier is less than ¾ inch (2 cm) tall.

To enjoy the art fully, people have to understand the nuances and depth of the compositions. A brief look hardly begins to capture the pleasure of the works.[4] Starting from the foot of the mini-mountain, then looking up to its top, the viewer first gazes at the frontal view before moving to look at the right side. Going slowly around the work, the viewer will examine carefully what is added to the mountain and its surroundings, observing whether each figure or shape is a representation of legend or of fact. These representational items are intentionally bigger in scale than other items in the scene. The viewer will evaluate whether the reduced form is in scale and balanced or out of scale and imbalanced, and he or she will perhaps read the intentions of the builder. For instance, if the builder wished to show his thankfulness to his wife, he would attach an egret somewhere in the mountain because an egret represents a devoted wife sacrificing her own interests for the good of her husband and children. She has to work hard to have enough food for the family and enough money for expenses while her husband is away at war. Adding to the wife's burdens is the husband's old and helpless mother who needs care. The Vietnamese woman's deeds are extraordinary, as expressed in these lines of Vietnamese folk poetry:

> Cái cò lặn lội bờ sông,
> Gánh gạo đưa chồng, tiếng khóc nỉ non.
> Nàng về nuôi cái cùng con,
> Để anh đi trẩy nước non Cao Bằng.
> Chân đi đá lại dùng dằng,
> Nửa nhớ Cao Bằng, nửa nhớ vợ con.[5]

[The egret is seeking food along the river shore
The wife, taking leave from her husband, cries even more
At home; she'll have to take care of her children and mother
While her husband is to fight the war at Cao Bằng.
At the parting moment, the husband looks back:
Duty awaiting in Cao Bằng conflicts with love for family.]

Using symbolism, the Vietnamese people have expressed their views through the years by carving many pictographic wooden boards. The main subject or figure is always largest in size. Similar techniques may be used in Hòn Non Bộ or Tiểu Cảnh (the art of miniscenes). When the artist wants to emphasize the plants, he uses plants that are larger and out of proportion. In the older carved pictographs on wood, which tell stories of Ngô Quyền defeating the Hán invaders or of Trần Hưng

Đạo breaking the conquering hold of the Mongolians during the Yuan dynasty, the subject characters are always bigger than the enemies. This is to emphasize the heroic and brave characteristics of the generals who considered enemies to be little children who were easy to defeat. More recent works are proportional.

Two approaches are used in creating works of miniature landscape art. The first is to reproduce a natural landscape in miniature, such as Hạ Long Bay, Yên Tử mountain, Hương Tích and Phong Nha caverns, Ngũ Hành Sơn mountain range, or Hòn Phụ Tử in Hà Tiên.

The second is to illustrate stories from Việt Nam's history by creating unusual forms and shapes in accordance with classical artistic rules or using legendary themes, such as Phượng Vũ (Phoenix Dancing), Phượng Ấp (Phoenix Hatching), Cửu Long Tranh Châu (Nine Dragons Fight for a Pearl), Long (Dragons), Lân (Heavenly Dogs), Qui (Turtle), and Hình Nhân Bái Tướng (An Old Fisherman Prays for Good Weather). Other themes denote a way of life, such as Mẫu Tử Tình Thâm (Love of a Mother for Her Child), Hòn Vọng Phu (Wife Awaiting Husband)—in Việt Nam, there is a famous mountain with a silhouette that appears to be that of a wife holding a child, waiting for her husband—or Tam Cương (Three Duties of Women). (The three duties of women are to listen to their father before they are married, to listen to their husband after they are married, and to listen to their firstborn son after they are widowed.)

Ngũ Hành Sơn (Five-Element Mountain) is a religious theme representing five different things to three different religions:

Taoism: the five elements of metal, wood, water, fire, and earth.

Confucianism: the five virtues of benevolence, righteousness, civility, knowledge, and loyalty.

Buddhism: the five commandments of Buddha against murder, theft, lust, lying, and drunkenness.

Like other forms of art, Hòn Non Bộ reflect the feelings and emotions of the artists, including cultural as well as personal feelings. Titles are not necessarily literal, and the artwork is not necessarily representational.

The Westerner who may be surprised at the nature of some of the themes expressed in this art should stop to consider how many times he or she has seen representations of the cow jumping over the moon or the wolf dressed in grandmother's clothing attempting to convince Little Red Riding Hood that all is well.

To understand why the artist may have made the shapes and forms that he has, one must know that traditionally, the builder of a Hòn Non Bộ was supposed to obey these five "Don'ts:"

1. Don't leave openings that allow the viewer to see through the Hòn Non Bộ, through the mountain itself.
2. Don't make the main mountain as small as others in the group. The principal subject must be the biggest to distinguish the host and the guests, the main and the auxiliary mountains.
3. Don't cut or split the top of a mountain or make it flat or sharp. The top of the mountain must be angular. In other words, it should look as natural as possible.
4. Don't make a dead end. There should be some way for the inhabitants, real or imaginary, to have access and to withdraw, even if it is a single path.

Detail of Hòn Non Bộ (Mountain Reflections)

73

5. Don't make the work out of proportion. Remember, any houses, temples, human figures, or animals placed in the work must be proportional to the size of the whole work, and the location of these items must be proper. For instance, the fisherman cannot be sitting on top of the mountain, nor can a deer be near a tiger. In short, the arrangement of any item in the work must be logical, realistic, and pleasing to the eye.[6]

These old "Don'ts" may be broken to convey additional meanings. A mountain intentionally made with an opening that can be seen through implies the builder is looking for honest people. When the mountaintop is intentionally cut or split, it implies the builder wishes to find a person who is able to understand him.

Present-day miniature landscape art is very creative and does not always follow the classical rules so closely. Hòn Non Bộ can be made simply to please the

Detail of Hòn Non Bộ (Egrets Returning Home)

Detail of Hòn Non Bộ (A Foggy Morning)

builder. It can be based on a legend, a true story, or an imaginative story, or it can just be a reminder of something not to be forgotten. It can also be a reflection of beliefs and ideology. A builder does not have to copy exactly what is seen in nature or strictly follow standards set by others, although he or she should refer to the fundamental guidelines to create a composition rich in form and style.

Notes

1. Lê Văn Siêu, *Văn Minh Việt Nam* (Vietnamese Civilization), Xuân Thu, Los Alamitos, California, 1989, p. 316.

2. Nhất Thanh và Vũ Văn Khiếu, *Đất Lề Quê Thói* (Local Custom and Tradition), Đại Nam, Glendale, California, 1976, pp. 245–246.

3. Toan Ánh, *Các Thú Tiêu Khiển Việt Nam* (The Many Hobbies of Việt Nam), Mũi Cà Mau, Cà Mau, Việt Nam, 1993, pp. 79–87.

4. Toan Ánh, *Các Thú Tiêu Khiển Việt Nam* (The Many Hobbies of Việt Nam), Mũi Cà Mau, Cà Mau, Việt Nam, 1993, pp. 79–87.

5. Nguyễn Văn Ngọc, *Tục Ngữ Phong Dao* (Proverbs and Folk Poetry), volume 2, Sống Mới, Sài Gòn, Việt Nam, 1979, p. 40.

6. Hùynh Văn Thới, *Kiểng Cổ và Chậu Xưa* (The Ancient Styles of Miniature Plants and Pots), Youth Publishing House, Thành phố Hồ Chí Minh, Việt Nam, 1996, pp. 110–111.

Additional Reading

Nguyễn Đăng Thục, *Lịch Sử Tư Tưởng Việt Nam* (The History of Vietnamese Ideologies), Thành phố Hồ Chí Minh, Việt Nam, reprinted 1998, volume 1, pp. 87–108.

Hòn Non Bộ in Balboa Park Botanical Building, San Diego, a gift from the Vietnamese people of San Diego to visitors of the park.

CHAPTER FOUR

Creating a Hòn Non Bộ

Hòn Non Bộ is a complete natural mountain landscape reduced in
scale, often with full, lush vegetation.

What Is Different about Hòn Non Bộ?

To make Hòn Non Bộ, you should keep in mind the features that make Hòn Non Bộ
different from other forms of living art. In bonsai, the emphasis is on the trees, usually one to a pot; a mountain may be represented by *suiseki,* a separate art form,
and other vegetation is represented by an accessory plant. The three elements of
tree, rock, and plant suggest a natural landscape in a sparse, minimalist approach.

In the past, Chinese penjing has made relatively little use of actual water, instead using features that symbolize water; Hòn Non Bộ uses real water that usually
represents the shallow sea around mountainous islands. Rock penjing may feature
interesting rocks, intricate and excellent abstract forms, but not necessarily in the
shape of mountains. In Hòn Non Bộ, the rocks are always arranged to look like a
mountain or range of mountains, or a mountainous island in the sea.

The long-term historical use of concrete containers is unique to Hòn Non Bộ.
Bonsai and penjing use ceramic and marble containers, though some containers are
made of other materials. The size of most Hòn Non Bộ precludes the use of ceramic containers; the white color of marble stains over time and does not set off the
mountain scenery of Hòn Non Bộ nearly so well as the dull-colored concrete con-

Front view of the main mountain in the Hòn Non Bộ in Balboa Park Botanical Building. Hòn Non Bộ must look good from all sides.

Detail of the top of the main mountain showing the crevices and caves in the Hòn Non
Bộ in Balboa Park Botanical Building.

tainers. White would seldom if ever be used, as it is associated with death in Vietnamese culture.

Bonsai and penjing are usually designed to have a front, a side from which the tree or the stones look best. Hòn Non Bộ are designed to be seen from all sides, so the builder must make all four sides look good. Bonsai are displayed so the viewer can look into the center of the tree; Hòn Non Bộ are displayed so the viewer can

Right side of Hòn Non Bộ in Balboa Park
Botanical Building. Note that the vegetation
stops short of the top of the mountain.

Detail of the right side of the Hòn Non Bộ in Balboa
Park Botanical Building showing a tiny waterfall dripping from the top of the opening in the rock on the left.

look down on top of the display as well. The mountain must look good not just from four sides but also from the top.

Hòn Non Bộ, then, generally represent a complete mountain scene, most often an island mountain scene, in a shallow concrete container with water to represent the sea. Bonsai is half design and half horticulture. Hòn Non Bộ require the artist to be a sculptor as well as a designer and a grower.

The back view of Balboa Park Hòn Non Bộ,
which is as attractive as its front view.

At the back of the main mountain of the Balboa Park Hòn
Non Bộ there is a small boat and a hut on the island.

The Hòn Non Bộ pictured in the first part of this chapter was donated to Balboa Park in San Diego by the Hòn Non Bộ Association to introduce a part of Vietnamese culture to the people of the United States. All four sides of the scene are shown, as are the details from each side. Notice the use of a shallow basin with glass on the sides; this enables the viewer to see the plants and rocks placed below the surface of the water.

Left side of Hòn Non Bộ in the Botanical Building in Balboa Park. No matter which side the composition is viewed from, the overall shape is that of a pyramid.

The left side of the main mountain of the
Hòn Non Bộ in Balboa Park. The tiny waterfall is more clearly visible from this side.

Selecting the Scene

Before starting a Hòn Non Bộ, the builder must have in mind the scene to be realized. There are two choices: natural and imaginative scenes. Whether the scenes are beautiful or not depends upon the skill of the builder.

When depicting a natural scene, the builder may copy what he or she sees in nature and reproduce it in a shallow container. When creating an imaginative scene, the builder can be on his own. The builder must have a rich imagination to visualize the streams, the cliffs, the caverns, and the proper arrangement of each to make the whole scene lively and aesthetically pleasing. Like music or painting, this kind of work can reflect the innermost feelings of its creator.

Steps in Building a Hòn Non Bộ

Selecting the Rocks

Rocks are the essential material for constructing a Hòn Non Bộ. Two kinds of rocks may be used:

Hard rocks—pieces with many cracks along their cleavage and many hollows make the rocks look natural.

Soft rocks—these can be sawed or cut and carved to create the desired shape, and perhaps to make cavities for planting trees. Since soft rocks are water permeable, plants can grow easily on them.

Using many different kinds of rocks in one Hòn Non Bộ should be avoided, for they would not only make it look unnatural but also unrealistic and geologically inconsistent—generally, mountains do not have many different kinds of rocks in one place.

Rocks can be found in the desert, in rocky areas, in the mountains, along the shores of rivers and streams, and at rocky beaches where sea waves tap against them day and night, eroding the rocks into a great variety of sizes and shapes. When selecting rocks, one should pay attention to:

- Pieces in triangular forms
- Pieces that have the shape of high cliffs
- Pieces that can stand as bases of mountains
- Pieces that can be made into waterfalls
- Pieces that look like many mountain peaks coalescing into one

- Pieces that can be made into steep walls
- Pieces that can be made into promontories

Pieces that are smooth or flat, and thus show wear, or those that are less interesting should be put under a stream or behind a waterfall.

Rock-Carving Techniques

If a piece of rock must be carved into a shape, the builder should take advantage of the cracks along the cleavage of the rock. He may have to carve along the cleavage of the rock, carve in traverse to the cleavage of the rock, or carve freely, to produce a cavern or a hanging rock over a body of water.

The second series of photographs in this chapter illustrates the carving techniques used to create the Hòn Non Bộ of Hòn Phụ Tử (Father and Son Island) in south Việt Nam, shown in chapter 1. The material for the miniature mountains is feather stone, a lightweight volcanic material available in landscaping material centers. It is very sharp, and gloves should be worn when working with the rock; eye protection and dust filters or masks should also be worn when working with feather stone.

Rock-Cementing Techniques

By cementing them together, you can assemble smaller rocks to permanently create a larger mountain. Both epoxies and cement-based mortars can be used to fas-

Raw material: two pieces of feather stone. Feather stone is a very lightweight volcanic material that must be handled carefully because it is so sharp.

Cutting a flat bottom on the large stone. Since the bottom
will be hidden under water it does not matter that it is cut.

Large rock divided and the initial grouping formed. A good deal of trial and
error may be involved in arriving at the proper arrangement of the mountains.

ten rocks together. Before the advent of epoxy and cement, Vietnamese artists would burn limestone to get material to use in mortaring stones together.

Once the pieces of rocks have been selected, they should be cleaned with a metal brush to remove all dirt and stains, then washed completely before being cemented together. Use a good premixed cement-and-sand mortar mix (they are carried by most hardware or construction-material stores). Pure cement is not recommended because it can break easily. Some color should be added to the mixture to match the rocks. Big pieces of rocks should be laid at the bottom, smaller ones on top. Use copper wire or other material to hold pieces in position after applying mortar. After five to ten minutes, use a spray bottle to wash off some of the outside cement coat so the joints look more natural, neither too smooth nor too grainy. Small fragments of rock can be applied to the outside of the cemented areas. Two to three days later, the binding wire can be removed and the upper parts of the mini-mountain built up gradually with the same pattern. Be careful not to cement so many stones together that they form a large piece too heavy to move.

In the final picture of the Father and Son Hòn Non Bộ in chapter 1, the right-hand

The Father and Son Hòn Non Bộ when it is about 70 percent complete. Although still rough, the outlines of the father and son arrangment are becoming apparent, and the taller, thinner rock has been moved to the left side.

mountain (the father) and the stone on its immediate left are fastened together with epoxy. As the feather stone was worked to form the two main mountains, smaller pieces were separated and used to make the jumble of rocks at the foot of the two mountains. Sometimes, pieces of the jumbled rocks were epoxied together; in other instances, they were just set in place.

The stone was further worked to create fissures and crevices in the rock, and the small pieces of rubble were given similar grain and patterns. The composition was tested in a concrete tray with water to see how close it was to the real thing. When compared to a photograph of the original, the two mountains appeared too wide, so further cutting was done. To get a reflection in the water similar to that in the photograph of the natural scene, the composition was set as far back in the tray as possible for the final photograph. Refer back to the photo in chapter 1 to compare the completed reproduction with the original landscape.

The Father and Son Hòn Non Bộ when it is about 90 percent complete. Place the rocks in the water to help establish the final placement and proportions of the rocks.

Mini-Mountain Groupings

With one exception which we will explain—that four mountains cannot be used—artists are free to choose their own styles and make their own groupings of mountains.

One-Mountain Hòn Non Bộ

A one-mountain Hòn Non Bộ can be either a single mountain or a group that has the principal mountain aligned with two or three smaller mountains. The group is built in a square, hexagonal, octagonal, or round basin. The mountain is placed in the center of the basin because the Hòn Non Bộ must look good from all sides; placing

Although the mountain peak is directly over the center of the pot, the mountain looks unbalanced because of the extra mass at the top right.

the mountain off center would cause one or more sides to be less attractive. Asymmetry and then balance are introduced with the placing of plants, small stones, and figures.

In the one-mountain scene shown here, the highest point of the mountain is positioned almost exactly over the center of the octagonal pot. The right side of the pot looks full and the left side empty. The addition of a tree to the left side and small bamboo-like grasses to the right side brings balance to the composition. The water and the egrets create a complete island scene that might very well be seen in Hạ Long Bay. Careful study of the trees on the left and right makes it clear that these are not designed in any of the classical styles of Japanese bonsai. Rather, the trees have a wild, falling-down, shaped-by-gravity-and-weather look.

Not only does the positive space occupied by the tree on the left add balance, but the negative space outlined by the tree also adds weight to the left side.

The stone used in this Hòn Non Bộ is tufa, a soft limestone from central California. The karst mountains in China and Việt Nam are also limestone. Tufa works easily, is porous enough that moss will grow on it, and yet resists wear and tear. The Hòn Non Bộ shown here could also be described as a cavernous mountain since it has many pockets and one opening that goes all the way through the mountain.

Two-Mountain Group

Two separate groups of mountains—one principal group and one auxiliary group—are placed in a rectangular or oval basin to create a two-mountain group. Traditional Vietnamese Hòn Non Bộ usually were not placed in oval basins; each side of the oval had a semicircle added to it to create a shape somewhat like a quince flower-shaped bonsai pot.

Although both authors prefer Hòn Non Bộ with odd numbers of mountains, a two-mountain group is presented here. The main mountain in this display was subsequently broken accidentally and, like the phoenix, was resurrected as a bird. It is now the center mountain in the Hòn Non Bộ identified as "Cockatiel Islands" shown in the photo Gallery in chapter 12. The birds in that Hòn Non Bộ are not phoenixes; only one of those birds exists at a time.

Three-Mountain Group

In three-mountain groups, three individual mountains or three groups of mountains with different sizes and shapes stand separately from one another in a rectangular or oval basin. The stones are placed and their lines established before any planting occurs. Small rocks may be placed around the bases of the mountains to change their mass and to serve as small islands and places to hide the roots of plants to be added later.

Four-Mountain Groups

Four-mountain groups are not used, since the number four is thought to be unlucky. The number four represents the four phases of man's life: being born, becoming independent, becoming sick, and dying.

Five-Mountain Group

Five mountains or groups of mountains stand isolated from one another in a rectangular or oval basin. The mountains are of different sizes, with a main mountain, two secondary mountains not quite of the same height, and then two more even smaller mountains. In a shallow Hòn Non Bộ tray, the mountains represent

Two-mountain group. The finished composition of this mountain group is shown in the Hòn Non Bộ entitled "Waiting," which appears in the Gallery in chapter 12.

Three rocks in the shape of birds to be used in a Hòn Non Bộ entitled "Cockatiel Islands." Although the base of the two-mountain group was accidentally dropped, it has, with the use of mortar and epoxy, become the base of the center bird.

Main mountain of Bình Minh Ở Việt
Nam (Morning in Việt Nam).

the tips of peaks that start far beneath the surface rising up from the floor of the ocean.

Multimountain Range

A multimountain group has many mountains of different heights, sizes, and shapes put together in a range and placed in a rectangular or oval basin. Great care must

One of the two secondary mountains of Bình Minh Ở Việt Nam (Morning in Việt Nam).

be taken to avoid crowding too much in one container, so multimountain ranges are usually placed in very large containers.

Inclining mountain ranges are a variation of multimountain ranges. This type has all the mountains leaning in the same direction, as if they had been tipped up by some great upheaval of the earth.

The other secondary mountain of Bình Minh Ở Việt Nam (Morning in Việt Nam). The complete composition is shown in the Gallery.

Unusually Shaped Mountains

Some rocks have extraordinary shapes—resembling a human head, a dog, a chicken, a turtle, a bird, or some other animal—that are very suitable for miniature landscapes. In this case, a round, square, hexagonal, or octagonal basin is recommended.

A Cavernous Mountain

In the photo from Hòn Non Bộ Stone Bridge, note the small stone bridge spanning the front of the cavern at the base of the mountain. Note also how the small mountain on the left balances the composition. The use of negative space between the small and large mountains is important, although mountains are usually thought of as solid masses.

Hanging Mountains

Hanging mountains occur naturally where ocean waves have undercut the side of the mountain over time. They may also be created when carbonic acid in rain erodes the softer parts of a limestone mountain. A Hòn Non Bộ with a hanging mountain can be balanced with only a small mountain on the side facing the overhang.

Arranging the Mountains in a Basin

If the rock is soft and can be carved or added to easily, estimate the size of the mountain to be built before deciding on the size of the basin. Build the basin and then make the mountain. If the rock is hard and therefore difficult to work with, build the mountain before making a basin that fits it.

To ascertain the approximate size of a landscape with more than one mountain, first decide upon the size and height of the principal mountain. This principal mountain usually will be placed near either the left or right side of the basin. Smaller mountains will be placed on the opposite side for balance. For a multimountain range, the auxiliary mountains must be made smaller in size and should be slightly behind the main one. The smallest and simplest should be placed farthest from the main mountain to increase the apparent depth of the composition. The smaller the mountain, the farther away it appears to be.

If possible, lighter colored rocks should be used for the tops of the mountains since in natural light the tops of the mountains would appear lighter than the bottoms. Similarly, place lighter colored rocks in the background to increase the effect

Many stones can be viewed as different objects. This
unusual shape might represent either a fish swimming
from left to right or a duck swimming from right to left.

A cavernous mountain from the Hòn Non Bộ Stone
Bridge, which is shown in completed form in the
Gallery in chapter 12. Because the soft limestone
erodes so easily, there are many cavernous mountains in the natural landscape.

of apparent distance. Less detail is needed in the rocks in the background. Rocks with vertical lines make the mountains look taller; rocks with horizontal lines make them look wider. (Fashion-conscious people know these same visual effects apply to clothing.)

A hanging mountain carved to show how erosion has created its unusual shape.

To make the range look more natural, add more rocks at its foot. If a waterfall or a stream is desired, select a suitable place for it and insert a piece of soft rock in which a hole can be bored and a plastic tube inserted from behind and connected to a water pump (the pump can be purchased at any tropical fish store). If you use hard rock, put a plastic tube in position before cementing the pieces together. Big Hòn Non Bộ need big water pumps, which can be purchased at hardware stores.

Hòn Non Bộ with Waterfall in Dragon Basin, Ngọc
Sơn Temple, Hà Nội. Photo by Nguyệt-Mai Đinh.

CHAPTER FIVE

Making a Shallow Container

Originally in Việt Nam, basins for Hòn Non Bộ were carved from stones, then formed from stucco, followed by the use of concrete for the basins.

Using Concrete for a Basin

Although Việt Nam has clay and produces ceramic ware, the size of most Hòn Non Bộ precludes the use of ceramic trays. Clay has a tendency to shrink, warp, sag, and crack when made into large containers. Although concrete may shrink and even crack, it can be reinforced with steel and worked after drying to correct cracks and imperfections; it can also be made into most shapes that ceramic containers can be made into. Truly skilled artisans can make concrete containers nearly indistinguishable from ceramic containers.

Concrete or modern-day mortars containing no large rocks or aggregates, but rather fine sand and vinyl glue, are used for making the containers. With proper reinforcement, there is no limit on the size of the container that can be created, other than the need to be able to move it. It is not unusual to see a container that requires four people to move it.

In the photograph that opens this chapter, note the small waterfall and the intricate detail of the cast-concrete dragons on the basin of the Hòn Non Bộ at Ngọc Sơn Temple. The molds used to make such intricate designs were usually one-time molds that were destroyed in the process of removing them from the cured concrete. Use of modern rubberized and flexible molds permits reuse; however, it is not necessary to have such elaborate containers to enjoy Hòn Non Bộ.

Making a Basin

If a basin is to function both as a container for a miniature landscape and as an aquarium for fish (and therefore will be quite large), it is advisable to have a contractor build it. If a small basin for a small Hòn Non Bộ is part of a project for fun, start making a basin right after the mountain is done. Whether you build the basin or mountain first will depend on whether you have soft or hard rock. Because hard rock is difficult to carve and to change shape, build the basin to fit the mountain. Soft rock can be carved to fit an existing basin. Depending on the shape of the mini-mountain, the basin will be rectangular, oval, square, round, hexagonal, or octagonal. To make a basin or shallow container, follow these steps.

Measure
Arrange the mountain(s), together with any secondary stones, on a table and measure the widest part. At this time, decide whether plants will be placed around the edges of the container, and if so, add extra inches to the measurement to accommodate them. The array of mountains and rocks shown in the photo measures 25½ inches (64 cm) across; the inside diameter of the container will be approximately 30 inches (75 cm) across and the outside diameter 32 inches (80 cm). Relatively little extra space is left at the edge of the composition.

Make a Mold
A wooden mold is easiest to build; it takes relatively few tools and is inexpensive. The mold can be single (an outside mold) or double (an inside and an outside mold). For the edges of a single rectangular mold, four pieces of wood are cut to length. All four pieces should be beveled to a 20- to 25-degree angle to allow the basin to be removed from the form after the concrete has cured. The pieces are assembled together into a mold with screws. If the basin needs an outer lip, a notch can be cut in the top of the pieces to accommodate the reinforcing wire and concrete for the lip. Various types of wood can be used for the mold.

The photographs in this section show an octagonal mold being constructed. An ordinary table saw can be used to bevel the sides, cut the notch for a lip, and cut the angle of the ends—45 degrees for a rectangular mold and 67½ degrees for an octagonal mold. Accurate cuts are important; loose fits allow water to evaporate from the concrete and air to dry the corners of the casting more quickly than the rest of the container, sometimes leading to hairline cracks in the corners of the basin. Waterproof glue can be used to ensure there are no cracks in the wooden mold.

For a double mold, the procedures are the same, but the inner mold should be smaller than the outer one, leaving a gap of about ⅜ to ½ inch (9 mm to 1 cm) all the way around, which is the thickness of the basin wall. The inner mold needs a bottom and is placed inside the outer mold with the bottom down after mortar is troweled into the outer mold.

Depending on the size of the basin and the weight of the mountain, the bottom of the container should be about ½ to ¾ inches (1 to 2 cm) thick. The octagonal container shown here has a ½-inch (1-cm) thick bottom; it took 42 pounds (19 kg) of mortar to complete the basin and its feet.

Measuring for a one-mountain Hòn Non Bộ. Although this rock is soft and could have been carved to fit a pre-existing pot, the shape of the mountain was so right that a pot was created to fit the mountain.

Ripping the sides of a wooden mold at an angle—perhaps not a task for a beginner.

Rabbeting a notch to create a lip on the mold that the pot will rest on. Most cabinet shops will do this for a nominal fee.

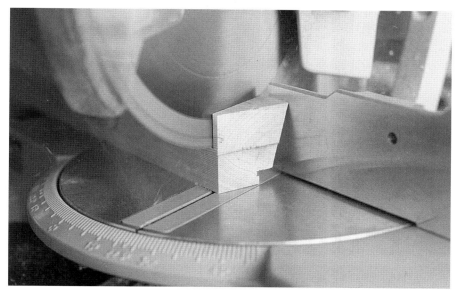

Mitering the end of a side piece of a mold. It is important that the pieces fit tightly together to avoid air spaces; therefore a good quality saw is a necessity.

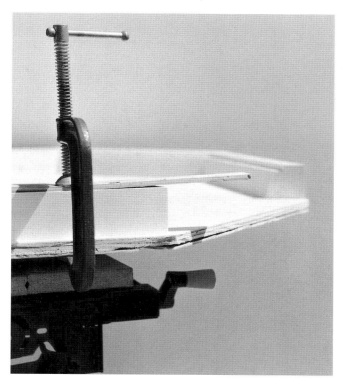

Gluing a side piece of the wood mold to the bottom of the mold makes for an airtight joint. Strength may be added by assembling the pieces with screws as well as glue.

Adding Reinforcement

Cut metal reinforcement such as chicken wire or mesh used for stucco reinforcement in the shape of the basin and place it inside the wood mold. At the top of the basin, an overlapping portion of reinforcement is made into a border to support the concrete lip and keep it from being cracked or broken off.

Make the Mortar and Put It in the Mold

It is easiest to use the premixed concrete or mortar mixes carried at construction material stores, including brands like Quikrete (Vinyl Concrete Patcher). To provide color for the basin, up to 4 pounds (1.8 kg) of coloring pigment (usually iron oxide and charcoal) should be added to a 40-pound (18-kg) bag of premixed mortar. Mix the pigment and mortar dry, and be sure to reserve enough mortar-and-pigment mixture to make the feet after mixing the mortar for the pot itself. Use chocolate as the primary color added, although other colors may be used. Two pounds of chocolate coloring and 2 pounds (0.9 kg) of black coloring added to 40 pounds (18 kg) of mortar produce a finished color about the same as the dull purple-brown of unglazed bonsai pots. The color of the mortar may also be matched to some of the rocks in the display, if desired.

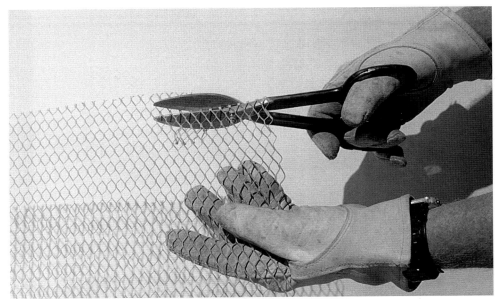

Cutting expanded mesh. Just as the concrete provides necessary bulk and form, the mesh is essential to add strength to the mold.

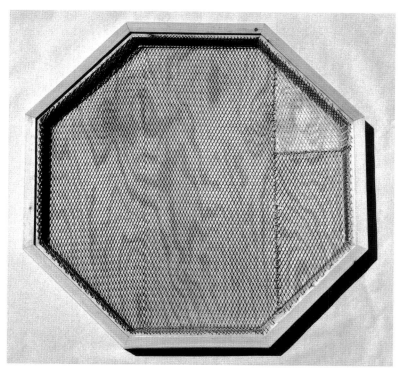

Expanded mesh cut into an octagonal shape. The mesh
should run up the sides of the mold as one of the weakest
places in the pot is at the joint of the bottom and the side.

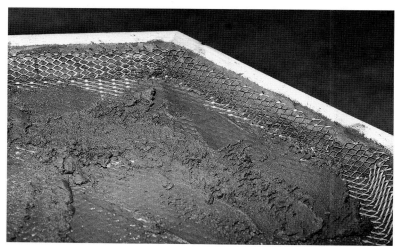

The first layer of mortar has been troweled into the mold,
and the expanded mesh reinforcement is added; a second layer of mortar is being started on top of the mesh.

Water should be added in accordance with the instructions to make the mixture workable but not wet. Too much water makes the mixture difficult to hold in place; too little makes it hard to fill in the gaps or corners. If two molds (an inside and an outside mold) are used, the mixture should be slightly wetter than if only an outside mold is used.

Approximately half of the mortar should be applied to the mold initially, then the wire reinforcing is inserted, and then the other half of the mortar is added. While there are techniques for holding the reinforcing in the center of large commercial concrete works, these do not work well with small pieces; hence the need to insert the reinforcement manually in the center of the concrete and then not disturb it by overworking.

Add Feet

When the basin is about three to seven days old, remove it from the mold and turn the basin upside down. Mark the bottom of the concrete basin with chalk to show where the feet will go. Use thin pieces of wood to make four molds in the shape of an L or a rectangle; metal molds can also be used. Brush a concrete bonding adhesive onto the basin where the feet will be attached, let the adhesive become tacky, set the molds in place, and fill them with mortar to create the feet. Feet may be reinforced with wire mesh for extra strength.

The second half of the mortar has been added and left to set up slightly before final troweling. Troweling too soon brings water to the surface of the concrete, weakening it.

Finish the Surfaces

If the basin is not as smooth as you want, use a Carborundum stone for smoothing; these are available in stores carrying concrete supplies. When the feet are completed and the pot is as smooth as you want, you may want to apply a thin layer of Concrete Crack Seal mixed with color to the outside of the basin to fill in any bubbles or defects.

Bonding adhesive is applied to the underside of the pot where metal molds for the feet will be placed. Wire mesh that is used to strengthen the feet is cut to shape. Feet must be reinforced as they will carry the weight of the pot.

After the feet are filled with mortar they are troweled smooth. Various materials can be used for the molds of the feet; in this case, metal strapping from a crate was used.

Working with Concrete

A few notes on working with concrete and mortar will help the novice. Be sure to add water to the mortar strictly according to the instructions on the bag, not based on instinct. The mix should be relatively stiff and able to stand up when piled up with a trowel. In commercial concrete work, a slump test is done to see that the mix does not contain too much water. While wetter concrete is easier to force into a mold, the excess water will evaporate and cause shrinkage in the finished piece.

Use a wooden float or trowel for the first rough passes, especially when using only an outside mold to make the basin. Metal trowels produce a smoother product, but working concrete with a metal trowel too soon brings excess water to the surface and will result in a weaker product, sometimes causing the surface to flake off. Overworking concrete will do the same thing; work the concrete or mortar just enough to get the shape and finish you need.

A green or uncured pot after it has been removed from its mold.

Brush oil on the molds before using them; cheap motor oil works well for this purpose. This will prevent water from soaking into the wood and will allow the concrete casting and wood mold to separate more easily. Oil the mold at least twenty-four hours before using it so that no or very little oil will adhere to the concrete when it dries. Re-oil the mold each time before using it. A properly made mold can be used twelve to eighteen times before the wood fibers begin to separate and leave an impression on the casting.

If possible, after the final troweling cover the entire piece with vinyl or a large piece of shrink-wrap to control the evaporation of the water. Rapid evaporation results in cracks (they must be filled in later) that do not always disappear even when filled. If the mold has cracks in it where air can enter, fill the cracks with

A color-coated pot with one mountain in it. Small islands and stones are placed within an inch (2.5 cm) of the edge of the pot; a larger pot would allow the eye to wander further away from the main subject.

plastic wood or epoxy before you use it to prevent rapid evaporation of water at those points.

Unless you are a skilled concrete worker, do not use rapid-setting mortar since it will not give you time to work the material into place. Do not be in a hurry to put stress on the basin by placing the rocks and water in the container before it has had sufficient time to dry and set. Concrete achieves approximately 95 percent of its strength in the first two weeks of curing and the remaining 5 percent very slowly over time.

One final note on the mold itself. Plywood (used for the base) sometimes has a torsional twist. If the finished mold is not flat because of a twist in the plywood base, correct it by clamping the mold to a flat surface to make sure the bottom of the mold is flat and in the same plane. Otherwise, one corner of the resulting pot will be higher than the others, the legs will not sit evenly on a flat surface, and the pot will rock. If the legs do not sit perfectly flat, place precut wooden wedges or shims under them when the mountains are added, to make sure all legs bear their share of the weight and to reduce the chance of creating hairline fractures in the pot due to uneven weight distribution. Should such fractures occur, they can usually be fixed with Concrete Crack Seal colored to match the pot.

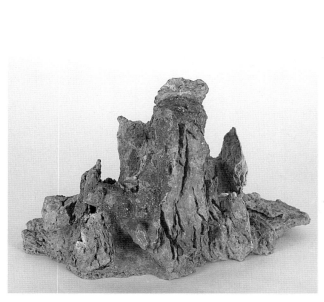

A base of a mountain that has been correctly carved and formed.

A main mountain as it should appear.

An arch is added to allow water to flow between two mountains, so connecting them as it would in nature.

Once all the pieces are properly in place they are ready to be measured for a container.

CHAPTER SIX

Common Errors
in Building Hòn Non Bộ

Hòn Non Bộ is landscape reduced to scale.

ALTHOUGH THERE ARE NO STRICT RULES about the proper proportions for the respective elements of a Hòn Non Bộ, the key factor to focus on is balance. Historically, artists have suggested that compositions should be divided into four parts water, three parts mountain, two parts land, and one part plants. Following a formula, however, places limits on creativity; artists must use their own judgment as to the right proportions. Earlier in the book we have provided descriptions and photography showing how to create a balanced Hòn Non Bộ composition, but sometimes it is instructive to show what *not* to do—the obvious errors make it clear what the correct course of action should be. Several pictures in this chapter are intended to show the beginning artist some pitfalls and how to avoid some common mistakes that may be made in building Hòn Non Bộ.

Do not have any trees taller than the mountain (except in the miniscene in which the main subject is the tree) because the mountain must symbolize greatness and gorgeousness. Note also that the tree serves as a backdrop for the mountains. In Tiểu Cảnh, or miniscenes, the tree is the main subject and is therefore larger than the mountains, with the mountains serving as a backdrop for the tree.

Do not use egrets or other birds that are larger than human figures, pagodas, temples, bridges, or other items such as houses and fishing boats in the composition. They will look out of proportion. If, however, an egret and a man are on different

The tree overwhelms the mountains because the
mountains are not small enough to appear as if
they were in the distance. The tree should also
not be placed at the very top of the mountain.

The egret is too large compared to the
boat. Proper proportions are essential to
create the illusion that the scene is natural.

sides of the mountain and are in proportion to the rest of the items on their respective sides, it is appropriate to use different-sized figures.

Do not arrange the principal mountain and the auxiliary one in conflicting directions. This causes the viewer's eye to follow diverging lines, leading attention away from the composition rather than back to it.

Do not build too many mountains in one cluster or plant too many trees on them or the Hòn Non Bộ will appear a cluttered pile of rocks or plants.

Do not place the principal mountain farther back than the auxiliary ones, restricting the imagination of the viewer. The viewer should bring his own imagination into play, perhaps thinking of valleys and ravines that may lie behind the main mountain.

Do not make the bottom of the mountain narrower than its top, which makes the mountain look unnatural and unstable. While hanging mountains may look as if a portion might fall off, they do not look like they are going to fall over.

Do not build the foot of the auxiliary mountain wider than that of the main one. A geological upheaval would have pushed the taller mountain higher and it therefore needs a broader base to support its height.

Mountains that point away from one another direct the eye away from the composition. The viewer does not know which way to look and so feels somewhat confused.

121

Mountains that point toward one another correctly lead the viewer's eyes toward the center of the composition, which is where the artist wants the viewer to look.

The tray is very crowded because there are too many mountains too close together; it looks like a jumble of stones.

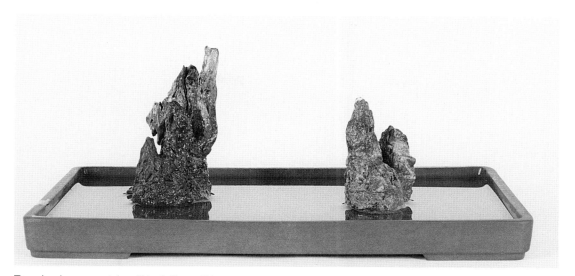

Too simple a mountain will look like nothing more than a piece of rock. Such a sparse display of mountains will not engage the viewer very long.

A correct display requires that the largest mountain be placed toward the front of the container. Placing smaller mountains toward the back increases the apparent depth of the composition.

The mountain is unstable and it looks unnatural; it would look better if the top and bottom were inverted. There is also no apparent geographical reason for the shape of the mountain, and therefore it would be an unnatural feature in the landscape.

Taller mountains need broader bases to support their height. While some variations are used, mountains are generally shaped in a pyramid form.

Do not make all the mountaintops the same height. In all visual compositions, there are horizontal lines; to balance that and relieve the monotony, vertical relief is required. Mountaintops of the same height create another horizontal line, and the balance between horizontal and vertical is not proper.

Do not plant a tree on the very top of the mountain. If there is a good opening in the rock near the top, you may plant a tree there, but then place an additional rock on top so that the tree is not at the highest point. It would be unnatural for a tree to grow at that location.

Here are some suggestions for creating a pleasant composition:

Look at nature around you and use it as a model. If you don't have mountains close by, study books. Pictures of the high karst mountains in China as well as Việt Nam can serve as models. People in other countries may look to their own mountainous regions for inspiration.

Use smaller egrets, houses, and objects near the tops of mountains and larger ones at the bottom because this helps create the illusion that the tops of the mountains are far away. Nothing should be placed at the top of the main mountain, but egrets can be positioned at the tops of smaller, secondary mountains.

Use larger trees at the bottom of a mountain and smaller ones farther up. Use trees with dark green foliage at the bottom and trees with lighter green foliage to-

The unvarying height of the mountains is uninteresting. The even tops also create a second horizontal line that, together with the horizontal line of the pot, overwhelms the vertical aspects of the display.

ward the top and the back. Both techniques give the impression that the mountain is tall and in natural light at the top and in shadow at the bottom.

Place subsidiary rocks at the base of the mountains so that any three rocks together form a scalene triangle—that is, a triangle in which no two sides are equal. Avoid the regular, evenly placed look that could occur because that does not appear natural.

Place smaller rocks at the back to represent mountains in the distance. This increases the apparent depth of the composition.

Consider the ratio of four parts water, three parts mountain, two parts land, and one part plants, and use only enough plant material to suggest forests, jungles, or marshes.

The tree has no protection from the wind. If a tree survived at the top of a mountain, the wind would blow it horizontal or even into a drooping position.

The tree is now sheltered and can grow erect in the lee of the rock. It can grow partially erect with some of its branches cascading or hanging down the side of the mountain.

Use handmade objects with discretion, and remember that they are representations. To the Western eye, small figures in the landscapes may seem incongruent, but to the Asian eye, the small figures are symbolic and complement the composition. An egret symbolizes the faithful wife in Việt Nam; in other Asian cultures it symbolizes longevity. Two scholars playing chess symbolize a serene, contemplative way of life.

Juniperus Procumbens 'Nana'

CHAPTER SEVEN

Trees on Hòn Non Bộ

Some of the mountains in Việt Nam are heavily covered with trees; others have very few pockets of soil and only a few trees manage to live there.

Types of Trees

In East and Southeast Asia, conifers are usually found in high mountains where the weather is colder, and different kinds of ficus are found in lower areas or at the foot of the mountains where it is damp and warmer. Except for some huge Hòn Non Bộ, it is impossible to grow pines on a mini-mountain, since even the smallest pine may be so large as to ruin the proportions of the scene. The most suitable plants for Hòn Non Bộ are junipers and ficus. No tree should be planted on the top of the mountain, unless it is very small.

On the sparser mountains in Việt Nam, many of the trees seem to be falling down the side of the mountains. In large part, this is due to the fact that seeds can germinate in small pockets of soil, but as the trees become older and heavier, the roots are unable to hold the trees upright in the limited soil, so they begin to lean. Gradually the lean becomes more pronounced until finally the trees look as if they are ready to fall off the mountain.

When you look at the photograph at the beginning of this chapter, you will find that your eyes move up the mountain, then turn to the left at the top where the tree brings your eyes back down the left side to the base of the mountain from where they again go up the mountain, following an oval pattern of motion. Viewers are ordinarily not conscious of the fact that their eyes have been directed so, but the artist is well aware of the effect.

The tree in the opening photograph shows none of the careful branch placement that occurs in some bonsai. Nevertheless, it is right for this mountain because it looks as if the tree had grown in that position. In fact, the branches have been wired to position them, but not in the traditional cascade form found in bonsai. Branches are turned at awkward angles instead of smooth curves to mimic the appearance of trees that have had branches broken off and then grown new leaders. The foliage mass is slightly heavier at the top than at the bottom since the bottom branches quite likely would be weaker and thus not able to support as much foliage. Because the upper foliage melds into the mountain, the tree seems to be pointing strongly downward. If you draw an imaginary curve following the general outline of the foliage, it will end at the base of the mountain; the mountain will appear to have a broader base and to have increased its apparent mass.

A mountain pieced together, especially if from hard rock, may not have pockets that can hold moisture around the roots of a tree. If so, the tree should be planted in a plastic bag with moss and soil around the roots to retain some moisture and with holes punched in the bottom of the bag to allow for drainage. Some experimenting will be required to determine how small the plastic bag can be, how much moss and soil are required, and how often to water. Generally, daily watering is required.

The plastic bag should contain the moss on the bottom and then be filled with soil; there should be no air spaces because that would allow the roots to dry out. Watering with a hose or watering can that has a fine rose will avoid washing the soil away and carrying it down to the tray. It may be necessary once in a while to add

Concrete tray by Lew Buller. Several trees can be planted in a tray such as this, and it can be used in either Hòn Non Bộ or Tiểu Cảnh.

more soil or to replace a plant. Growing in such restricted conditions keeps the plant lean and sparse, but care should be taken not to overdo it. Instead, the artist should remove any plant that shows signs of stress and let it recover. Yellowing foliage generally indicates over-watering; graying or browning indicates under-watering. Either problem needs to be corrected immediately.

Mountains can be planted with a tree in the back and grasses in the front to create additional depth when the mountain is viewed from the front, as in the Hòn Non Bộ in this chapter. Such an arrangement is also in keeping with the principle that Hòn Non Bộ should look good from any side. *Juniperus procumbens* 'Nana' grows well in areas where little soil is available or where there is a moderate

A limestone mountain in a dry tray before the planting of trees and plants in the mountain's hollows and crevices begins. Placing stones in a tray, which is done first, is the more difficult task. Plants can be added or not as the need for balance requires.

The perforated plastic bag holds a clump of soil, moss, and tree roots together so they do not wash away when watered; the perforations allow excess water to drain away.

amount of water. To help the plant grow well, replace the soil each year and trim the tree's branches to the proper shape and proportion.

Boxwoods (*Buxus*), kishu junipers (*Juniperus chinensis* 'Kishu Shimpaku'), elms (*Ulmus*), figs (*Ficus*), and other small-leaved, water-tolerant trees may also be used on Hòn Non Bộ. In Việt Nam, ficus trees survive in the lower parts of the mountains, in part due to their ability to send out aerial roots. During hot, humid conditions, the aerial roots are stimulated to grow. When they reach the ground, they find pockets of soil and soon grow both to anchor the main tree and to extend the size of the canopy.

Việt Nam is a country of monsoons with essentially six months of hot, dry weather and six months of hot, wet weather. The trees on the mountains there must

A tree is planted below the top of the mountain where it looks more natural, especially since it has been shaped to hang over the side of the smaller mountain as if by the force of prevailing winds.

Adding a small *Juniperus Procumbens* 'Nana'. The size of the hand reveals just how small the tree is.

in early spring, may cling onto the leaves in bunches. Wash them off with a steady stream of water. To avoid harming other plants or fish, either do not use insecticides, or spray the trees before they are planted on the Hòn Non Bộ. If an insect problem persists, it may be best to replace the tree.

A healthy, small-leaved tree (*Ficus* spp.)
ready for planting in a Hòn Non Bộ.

A Vietnamese waiting house, where generals
and mandarins would wait to see the king. The
roof on a Vietnamese building curves up more
sharply than the roof on a Chinese building.

CHAPTER EIGHT

Adding to the Mountain

The builder may stimulate the viewer's imagination by not putting everything on the Hòn Non Bộ. A bonze walking up the mountain can tell the viewer that his pagoda is somewhere behind the mountain, that it cannot be seen from the front.

IN THE OLD DAYS, no accessories like fishermen, woodcutters, scholars reading books, cottages or pagodas, birds, or other animals were added to Hòn Non Bộ. Instead, the mountains themselves were made into the shapes of sacred animals such as dragons, heavenly dogs, turtles, and phoenix, or into the shape of a person in a pensive mood—a way of expressing the artist's feelings.

Later on, as Hòn Non Bộ tended to be copies of natural landscapes, items in the shapes of animals and birds were added to the mini-mountains. Buddhist temples were glued to the side of the mountain, or a bridge over a stream was created to enhance the landscape. Some religious people, depending on their beliefs, added statuettes of Buddha or of Jesus Christ and the Virgin Mary. Most frequently, the objects added are those that might be found in a country scene, such as huts, bridges, and boats.

Handmade Objects

The relationships between objects added to Hòn Non Bộ must be compatible. For example, a pagoda should be under the shade of a big tree. Wild animals like tigers

141

or bears or cougars must be on the rim of the mountain, and not near a house or other structure. An egret on the rim of a mountain must always be smaller than the one at the foot of the mountain. Such items are available in the market, but they are not made to scale. It is wise to select several sizes of each item to be able to match them harmoniously with others of proportionate sizes.

Many of the small handmade items added to Hòn Non Bộ are now made in China, but people familiar with Vietnamese and Chinese cultures will know the difference. For example, hats on the figures differ. Early Chinese wore their hair knotted at the top of their head, so their hats had a hole at the top to let the hair out. Vietnamese wore their hair knotted at the back of the head, so the hat was conical, with no opening at the top.

Bridges are a favorite addition and may be made of small stone slabs (rough-hewn), wood, bamboo, or ceramic in imitation of brick or stone with mortar. They may be used to connect two islands, a boat-landing spot to an island, two mountains, or two spots on a mountain trail that has been interrupted by a break.

Pagodas and temples are located throughout the Vietnamese countryside as well as in both small and large cities. They are found at different locations, many having been erected by officials of earlier dynasties. The size and style depend on the wealth of the builder and the degree of influence exerted by Chinese architec-

A country hut that has been hand painted by Nguyệt-Mai Đinh in traditional colors.

142

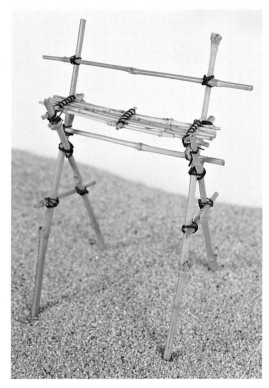

A bamboo bridge made by Nguyệt-Mai Đinh that is used to connect a span in a path that would otherwise be interrupted by a steep descent on one side and ascent on the other.

A Vietnamese ceramic bridge made to look as if it had been formed by logs; it is not as highly curved as Chinese or Japanese bridges.

A bamboo bridge connecting two mountains from the Hòn Non Bộ, Morning in Việt Nam. In spite of their fragile appearance, these bridges are very strong.

The curve of the rooftops marks this as a distinctly Vietnamese pagoda.

A gate to a walled compound that protected
kings, emperors, and other important people.

A gazebo from Việt Nam,
which is usually built
near a lake, where a king
could listen to music and
enjoy the view.

A hut with a fenced deck. The fence means that either the family has small children or that it is more affluent than most.

This boat made by Nguyệt-Mai Đinh is beached along the shore where a fisherman might have stopped to catch a small crustacean that resembles a crayfish.

A two-room hut built over water. Huts as large as these may have housed a family of four or more.

ture. The styles of the pagodas and temples were probably brought down from China as the Vietnamese were driven out from China to Việt Nam, and the changes to the Vietnamese styles of the pagodas and temples were made gradually.

Fishermen's huts and boats are found frequently in Hòn Non Bộ, as might be expected in an island scene. The huts are shelters from the weather; the boats are the transportation in the watery environment.

Humans and Animals

The innermost feelings of the builder of a Hòn Non Bộ may be inferred from the work itself. For instance, by adding a fisherman to the landscape, the builder might wish to express a desire to lead a secluded life. The fisherman sitting under a rock hollow by the stream implies that the builder wants to live near nature, disregarding worldly desires.

The only animal that is symbolic is the egret. The egret symbolizes the faithful Vietnamese wife, although this is not likely to be recognized by the nonVietnamese viewer.

Two egrets looking for small sea animals to eat. (Made by Nguyệt-Mai Đinh.)

Vegetation

The plants that grow well on Hòn Non Bộ generally need to be water tolerant. Rushes, reeds, and sedges, for example, grow very well either next to water or with their roots in water. Other kinds of plants that like water are baby's tears (*Soleirolia soleirolii*), *Scirpus cernuus* (syn. *Isolepis gracilis*), and dwarf papyrus (*Cyperus alternifolius* 'Gracilis'). These plants grow fast and need frequent care. Baby's tears may be attacked by leaf-feeding caterpillars. If baby's tears show signs of being eaten, search for the caterpillars and pick them out with tweezers.

The dwarf papyrus (*Cyperus alternifolius*) is called umbrella plant because its narrow leaves are arranged like the ribs of an umbrella. When used in a planting, its outline resembles that of a palm tree. When in the ground, the plant grows 2 to 4 feet (60 to 120 cm) tall. When grown in a pot, it is responsive to the amount of root space available; the smaller the pot, the smaller the plant. *Cyperus isocladus* (syn.

A ten-year-old miniature juniper (species unknown) that is small enough to be placed at the top of a mountain. It tolerates moisture and likes shade in the afternoon.

This nine-year-old *Buxus microphylla* var. *japonica* is 5 inches (12.5 cm) tall and, like all suitable Hòn Non Bộ plants, is fairly water tolerant. Since it grows so slowly, it can be left as a planting for many years without outgrowing its allotted space.

C. profiler) is also useful in Hòn Non Bộ because it too resembles a palm tree when the size is reduced from its normal height of about 18 inches (45.5 cm) when its root space is restricted.

Dwarf horsetail (*Equisetum hyemale*) grows slowly and tolerates much water. It is propagated by division; the plant shown in the photograph is the mother plant. Almost as tolerant as dwarf horsetail (*E. hyemale*) is the boxwood *Buxus microphylla* var. *japonica,* which tolerates very moist roots without rotting. It can also dry out somewhat without dying, and it even accepts the alkaline water of southern California.

Miniature sedges (*Carex* spp.) are extremely slow growing. Snails and slugs love to graze them down to their roots, but if the sedges are grown in a pan of water, which they are able to tolerate well, they will not be eaten.

The miniature bullrush (*Typha minima*) goes dormant once or twice a year. It propagates readily from seed (the miniature seedheads are visible in the photo) and is very moisture tolerant. It also prefers only morning sun.

Left: Cyperus alternifolius, approximately 6 inches (15 cm) tall. It grows easily from seed, and if planted in a very small pot will remain small.

Above: Dwarf horsetail (*Equisetum hyemale*), which resembles the small rushes found at the edge of rivers in Việt Nam.

149

Dwarf sasa bamboo (*Sasa* spp.) is a running type of plant that, in its natural setting, can grow 6 to 8 inches (15 to 20.5 cm) tall. To limit its growth, the plant is cut to the ground each January, and root space is restricted. It likes moist roots and some sun.

Many species and varieties of mosses are useful for Hòn Non Bộ. They may be placed around the roots of a tree to retain moisture, or they may be placed at the bottom of the planting hole to retain moisture for use by the roots of the tree. In addition, they may be used for groundcover.

The broad leaves limit the usefulness of most dwarf iris in Hòn Non Bộ. It likes sun and water, but blooms with great difficulty, and the bloom lasts only one day. *Erodium* (heron's bill) and *Alyssum* are two other flowering plants that, if managed, appropriately may also be added to Hòn Non Bộ. Alyssums in a starter pot will bloom when they are no more than 1 inch (2.5 cm) high. Because Việt Nam is so moist, even concrete will grow moss on it; the standing ground cover, if all else fails, should therefore be moss.

The rush *Scirpus cernuus* resembles bamboo in outline. It grows by seed or by division and can stand having its roots completely submerged in water; in fact, it grows better that way. Seeds spread easily by the wind and it will take over a garden if allowed to do so.

Above: A miniature Japanese sedge (*Carex* spp.) takes at least three years to achieve this size.

Right: Miniature bullrushes (*Typha minima*) with seedheads are very moisture tolerant.

Above: Dwarf iris, most likely the miniature dwarf bearded iris *Iris tenuifolia,* is very tolerant of water and often grows with its roots in water.

Dwarf sasa bamboo (*Sasa* spp.), about 2½ inches (6.5 cm) tall, will overrun a garden if left untrimmed. Some runners extend for several feet.

Scirpus cernuus (syn. *Isolepis gracilis*) is ideal for planting at the edge of the water where it grows easily and quickly.

Detail of Tiểu Cảnh (Two Deer by a Stream)

Tiểu Cảnh, A Miniscene

The Vietnamese people have long enjoyed the art of miniscenes and miniature plants, both of which have a close relationship to miniature landscapes.

What is a Miniscene?

The difference between a miniscene, or Tiểu Cảnh, and a miniature landscape, Hòn Non Bộ, is that in a miniscene the tree must be higher and bigger than the rock, which functions as a background for the tree. The rock may appear to be farther off in the distance because it is smaller than the tree. A miniscene is a snapshot of a natural scene, a part of a miniature landscape. Generally, a miniscene focuses on one feature of the whole panorama, such as a steep cliff, a cave, a beach, a bank of a river, a stream, or a lake. The tree in a miniscene is often bending, inclining, or growing downward. Trees have to be old, weather-beaten and faint.

To create a miniscene that pleases the eye, the builder must know how the rocks are to be pieced together so that they appear to be naturally deep and broad and even high, so causing the viewer to feel a sense of awe and grandeur. The pieces of rocks used for miniscenes have to be carefully selected; those with cracks or fissures along their grains are preferable. Sometimes the builder has to use a saw and chisel to form the pieces into desired shapes before cementing them together. The three rocks at the center of the scene in the photograph opening this chapter,

Tray with waterproof divider between the water and soil areas. Although some trees can survive roots that are constantly wet, most need an ample supply of air to their roots to aid in respiration.

Even though color may have been added to the mortar mix when the pot was made, it may not match the shade of rocks precisely, and a final coat of color can be applied to the tray.

for example, had to be shaped to fit so closely together. Rarely will rocks conform to one another this well without a little help from the artist. The viewer knows that rocks that fit together well in nature are the result of a volcanic upheaval that creates a mountain range; when rocks in a Tiểu Cảnh fit together so well, they give the illusion of having been created by nature rather than by man.

Round, oval, or rectangular basins are good for miniscenes. If the miniscene is a small beach or the bank of a stream, rocks should be arranged as an impermeable divider in the shallow basin; one side of the divided basin is filled with water and the other with soil. Darker colored rocks should be arranged near the tree, and those of a lighter color placed farther and farther away. The bottom of the section of the basin containing the soil, which is to be planted with trees, should have drainage holes so water can escape; otherwise, the tree will die. When planting a tree in a miniscene, the builder can use aluminum wire to hold the roots of the tree in the

Testing the pomegranate to see if it will fit; roots may have to be trimmed to make a tree fit, but if done at the right time, a third or more of the roots can be removed without damaging the tree.

155

desired position and keep it from falling down. On top of the soil, some kind of grass should be applied to hold the soil firm; the grass also enhances the beauty of the scene. Sometimes a little stream, similar to those in Hòn Non Bộ, is added to make the work more natural and lively.

A Tiểu Cảnh can be planted with trees, such as pomegranates, that have been in training in a bonsai pot. The need for porous soil that allows air to reach a tree's roots causes the soil to dry more quickly than it would otherwise, and therefore it must be watered more frequently than if it were in the ground. However, pomegranates do not generally like wet roots, and so the bottom of the planting area is

The pomegranate's roots are wired in place and covered with soil. The wiring stabilizes the tree in the pot until new roots can grow and create a solid foundation.

Detail showing hollow trunk of a pomegranate tree and alyssum in flower. Alyssum grows quickly and may need to be replaced, but it is inexpensive and generally available year-round.

filled with a coarse soil mixture, and a screen is placed over the drainage holes to keep the mixture from washing out. Above the layer of coarse soil mixture is a layer of free-draining potting mix, the same mix that will be worked down in between the roots when the tree is transplanted. If you want to grow moss, a top layer of about ⅛ inch (3mm) finely screened potting soil should be added. No attempt will be made here to provide the information necessary to grow bonsai; it is obvious, however, that the horticultural skills needed to grow bonsai will be very helpful to the beginning Hòn Non Bộ or Tiểu Cảnh artist.

Any figures or other items to be added to the miniscene must be proportional in scale to the scene as a whole. Grasses and ground cover, blooming or not, should be small-leaved. Manmade objects should be of a size that appears realistic.

A fully planted pomegranate in an unfinished Tiểu Cảnh. The light green color of the spring foliage on the tree is almost as pretty as the orange-red blooms that follow later in the year.

Types of Miniscenes

In Việt Nam, people enjoy four types of miniscenes. The first type consists of a plant placed in a shallow basin that can be filled with soil or water. It may include a piece of soft rock with a big hole in which the plant grows, or many small pieces of rocks can be cemented together to make a composite basin in which to grow the plant or mini-tree.

The second type consists of a plant grown on a rock. The roots of the plant cover the rock, reaching the soil that is on one side of the basin. The other side of the basin is filled with water, and the soil and roots are separated from the water by an impermeable divider.

In the third and simplest type of Tiểu Cảnh, a tiny tree is planted in a basin filled

A fisherman's hut that may be shared by one or more fishermen. Although water reaches the rocks, they keep the soil from washing away from the pomegranate's roots.

with soil, and many pieces of rock are laid around the tree. The fourth type of miniscene features many trees or plants, or many kinds of trees and plants. Some pieces of rock can be scattered here and there to make the view like a wild desert.

In any type of miniscene, the builder or owner must pay close attention to the trees, since they are the most important feature of this form of landscape art. The owner has to know when and how to trim the trees and which fertilizer to use so the trees will appear at their best.

Since the trees on Hòn Non Bộ are smaller than the mountains, and mountains in a Tiểu Cảnh are smaller than the trees, one must look at the entire scene to determine which it is.

As with Hòn Non Bộ, making and enjoying a miniscene requires an artistic sense, a rich imagination, great patience, and an everlasting passion for the art.

Moreton Bay fig (*Ficus macrophylla*) in training. It has very large leaves and requires aggressive pruning and restricted roots to keep the leaves in proportion to the branches and trunk. The aluminum foil holds soil around an aerial root.

159

Ficus benjamina in training
for use in a Tiểu Cảnh.

A hut set on a remote island that shows good use of
Scirpus cernuus (syn. *Isolepis gracilis*). The gulls,
which are less than one inch (2.5 cm) in wing span,
provide a good sense of proportion.

Right: The air is filled with gulls. This is a common scene, especially around a fisherman's hut where the birds look for scraps.

Below: Part of a finished Tiểu Cảnh. This scene is very much like those found in nature photographs in which a tree branch is used to frame the main subject.

Ulmus parvifolia, Chinese elm, in
training for use in a Tiểu Cảnh.

A close-up view of the left side of a Tiểu Cảnh allows a careful study of the elements that went
into making this particular Tiểu Cảnh.

A close-up view of the right side of a Tiểu Cảnh showing the weathered bark on the old elm. When it is transplanted, great care is taken not to touch the old bark.

165

A close-up view of old Chinese elm trees at the center of a Tiểu Cảnh. Old age in the plants used on miniature Vietnamese landscapes is highly valued.

Using an abrasive disk to
smooth the lip on a new pot.

CHAPTER TEN

Tools

In addition to tools used by most bonsai enthusiasts, tools for cutting and shaping rocks, some tools for woodworking, and tools for working and finishing concrete are needed to make a complete Hòn Non Bộ.

WHILE IT IS POSSIBLE to spend a great deal of money on tools, it is not necessary to do so. Improvising can add a great deal of fun to the process, and sharing tools with others interested in the art can keep it inexpensive.

Bonsai Tools

Although there are many specialized tools available for bonsai, such as branch splitters and jin-makers, only a few basic tools are needed to design and maintain the trees and accessory plants for Hòn Non Bộ. Concave cutters, knob cutters, and scissors are used for removing branches and trimming trees and plants. A root hook is nice at transplanting time, but bamboo chopsticks will do nearly as well, since most of the plants will be small and not require heavy root work. Wire in various gauges, annealed copper wire for conifers and aluminum wire for deciduous trees, is used to bend and shape branches and trunks. Aluminum wire alone can be sufficient; it is generally easier to acquire and can be reused readily. Aluminum wire can be unwound from trees, but annealed copper wire should be cut off. Specialized wire cutters are available, although ordinary wire cutters will suffice, especially if only aluminum wire is used.

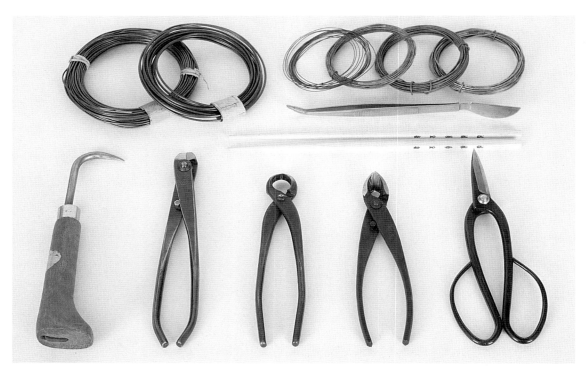

Basic bonsai tools. At the bottom from left to right are a root hook, wire cutters, a knob cutter, a concave cutter, and scissors. Above are chopsticks for working soil between the roots, and tweezers for removing weeds and excess leaves. At the top left is aluminum wire for use on deciduous or soft-bark trees; on the right is copper wire used on conifers.

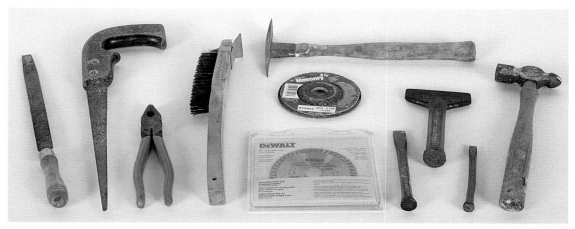

Various rock-cutting tools including, from left to right, a file, saw, pliers, wire brush, diamond and abrasive disks, chisels of various sizes, and two hammers.

Tools for Cutting and Shaping Rocks

Think safety. Working with rocks is more hazardous than working with plants. Rocks fracture, and broken pieces fly in all directions. A mask should be worn to avoid breathing in the dust that occurs from the cutting and finishing of the rocks. To prevent saws and chisels slipping and cutting one's hands, wear leather gloves. Don't take chances—acquire basic safety gear and use it.

Most hardware stores will have the tools necessary for working rock. Masonry chisels, new or used, hammers, wire brushes, and abrasive disks are readily available. One of the more unusual tools for rock work is an ordinary wood saw that will readily cut materials such as feather stone. If rocks are fastened together with mortar, a spray bottle with water and a small paintbrush are useful for removing excess mortar.

Using cutting disks in the same drive motor used for abrasive disks allows the artist to cut small rocks freehand; larger ones may need to be taken to someone with a full-sized rock-cutting saw. It is best to clamp a rock in place before cutting it. In the photograph of the rock being cut, the rock has not been clamped as that

At bottom left is a diamond-studded rock-cutting blade. To its right is a handheld stone cutter. Other items include basic safety gear such as, from top left, a face shield, ear protectors, and leather gloves.

Cutting a small rock with a cutting disk. The rock is not clamped because it is a very soft rock and the cut is being made from the top down. The blade should be rotating at full speed before you begin cutting any rock.

Often when a rock is cut at the right angle and at the right place, both the resulting pieces will become small islands that can be put to use in a miniature landscape.

would hide the cut from view. In that picture, the motor is not running and the blade is not moving, but the blade should be rotating at full speed before it begins cutting the rock, and all rocks, even soft rocks, should be held as immobile as possible. If a rock shifts, it may grab the blade and, at the very least, scare the user.

Mark the rock before cutting it, and see if a careful cut will permit both pieces of the cut rock to be used, which is often possible. The more interesting the uncut rock, the more careful the choice of cut should be.

Woodworking Tools

It may be possible to rent or borrow the larger, more expensive woodworking tools. The table saw and chop saw used to make the mold shown in chapter 5 were borrowed from a friend. (Actually, the friend cut the pieces while the pictures were being taken in exchange for some help in designing a garden.) Clamps, a drill motor and drill bits, and screwdrivers were all the remaining tools required to create the

Woodworking tools from left to right starting at the bottom typically include a cut-off saw, a cordless screwdriver, a manual screwdriver, a 16-ounce hammer, and a framing square. Above these are two C clamps separated by a bottle of water-resistant glue.

mold. Metal snips were used to cut the reinforcing mesh to shape. An old paintbrush and a tin can were used to apply inexpensive motor oil to the form.

The tools needed to make wooden molds for concrete pots are generally found in any toolbox. A table saw is a luxury, not a necessity; most cuts can be made with a circular saw and a cut-off saw. Fancy molds may require a band saw, but cabinetmakers often will make the cuts for a small fee—much less than the cost of a new saw.

Tools for Working Concrete

A minimal investment is required for concrete-working tools. A broad putty knife can be used to mix mortar and apply it to the mold; one or more small pieces of wood serve as the first floats to work the concrete down; a small rectangular hand trowel is used for finish-troweling. Plastic buckets can be used for water, clean-up, and mixing mortar.

Concrete-working tools. At the top and bottom of the picture are pieces of wood called striking edges. From left to right is a wooden float, a rectangular trowel, a second wooden float, a triangular trowel, and metal finish float. Above that is a small wooden float, and on the opposite side is a Carborundum stone for finishing hardened concrete.

Striking boards or striking edges are used to level the bottom of the pot before and after inserting the wire mesh. The notches on the ends of the boards are cut so the bottom of the deepest board is ¼ inch (6 mm) above the bottom of the mold and the bottom of the second board is ½ inch (1 cm) above the bottom of the mold. This permits two layers of mortar to be placed with the reinforcing mesh between the layers. The striking boards are sawed back and forth to level the mortar at the bottom of the pot.

Cleaning a pot with baby oil to get it ready for display.

CHAPTER ELEVEN

Displaying Hòn Non Bộ

In Việt Nam, Hòn Non Bộ are found almost everywhere—in train stations, public parks, offices, homes, and historic buildings.

ORIGINALLY, KINGS HAD Hòn Non Bộ built in their royal gardens. Later on, mandarins learned this form of art. It gradually spread to temples and pagodas, and finally lay people brought it into common practice. In the old days, Vietnamese people enjoyed Hòn Non Bộ privately as a principal form of entertainment and a major pastime. It was mainly for the retired, and rarely did they display Hòn Non Bộ in public.

The Art of Display

There is a fine line between issues of display and issues of composition. In Japanese-style bonsai, many conventions have been developed for displaying accessory plants and stones along with the bonsai themselves. Almost always, each item will be on a separate stand, and the shapes and sizes of stands vary within the display. Accessory plants change with the seasons; pot choices vary with the type of tree. In Hòn Non Bộ, plants, stones, and water are all in one pot (the size and shape of the pot will depend upon the type of mountain being displayed), so the conventions that govern the art relate to a single complex composition. The only seasonal changes are those that occur to the plants naturally.

Bonsai display and Hòn Non Bộ design share some of the same compositional conventions. The main item usually will be off-center, the pieces are not lined up in a straight row, and the positions of the secondary items—best described as having a "flow" coinciding with the primary item—are chosen to cause the viewer's eye to be directed back into the composition rather than out of it. Accessory plants, stones, and trees usually display what is referred to as "movement," and the movement of all items should be congruent, not conflicting, allowing the viewer to continue to look at the composition without being distracted by opposing flows.

Some more comparisons between Japanese-style bonsai displays and Hòn Non Bộ displays will demonstrate the differences between these forms of living art. The choice of pot is important to bonsai display; colored, glazed pots are used for flowering or deciduous trees, whereas unglazed, subdued pots are used for conifers. In Hòn Non Bộ, all pots are concrete. Well-to-do people may have Hòn Non Bộ pots with mosaic inlays in which pieces of broken ceramic are inlaid in the wet concrete of the pot to create images. Displays that contain fish in the water may use

A stand that is used to display Hòn Non Bộ on a patio or in another outdoor area.

178

a pot with a concrete base and glass sides so that the fish and aquatic plants can be seen.

Hòn Non Bộ pots may also have artwork painted on the wet concrete so that it becomes a permanent part of the material. Pots that are painted after the concrete is dry are seen not as artwork but rather as commercially produced pieces for sale. Paint on the inside of a pot may harm fish or plants, and so little paint should be used there.

In bonsai, the artist tries to match a tree with an existing pot following conventions based on trunk size and the height and width of the tree. Rarely is a pot designed for a specific tree. In Hòn Non Bộ, however, pots are usually designed specifically for individual mountains and usually stay with the composition throughout its life. In spite of this, it is possible to use parts of a composition in a different pot. For example, the Hòn Non Bộ captioned "Egrets Flying in the Sun" was created by using the main mountain from a Hòn Non Bộ entitled "A Foggy Morning."

An eight-sided basin on a stand in preparation for planting. The stand is almost exactly the same diameter as the pot so that the vertical rather than the horizontal elements of the composition will be emphasized.

The relative size of the items in both types of displays is important. Accessory plants and stones should be in proportion to the bonsai; in Hòn Non Bộ, plants, stones, water, and pots all must have pleasing proportions. An old rule for determining proportions for Hòn Non Bộ says that if a mountain is 13 feet (4 m) tall, the trees should be 16 inches (41 cm) tall, one-tenth as tall as the mountain. Animals should be less than 2 inches (5 cm), one-tenth as tall as the trees, and the people should be the size of a peanut.

Traditionally, Hòn Non Bộ are displayed in the round, without scrolls or backdrops. Bonsai, on the other hand, are often displayed both at home and in public with scrolls in the background, and when displayed in public, the backdrop is a light-colored one. In recent years, Hòn Non Bộ have sometimes been displayed with drawings of mountains as backdrops. If a backdrop is used in either bonsai or Hòn Non Bộ, it should be higher than the composition so the top of the composition does not extend above the backdrop.

Displays of bonsai and accessory plants may be chosen to suggest one of the four seasons of temperate zones; entire exhibits may be given over to shows of trees in their winter silhouette. In Việt Nam, there are two seasons, "hot" and "hot and wet." Consequently, the foliage on plants used in Hòn Non Bộ tends to be green and lush; ficus trees used on Hòn Non Bộ will have far more foliage left on them than their Japanese counterparts.

Japanese bonsai are divided into categories by size. For example, *mame* is small enough to hold in the palm of your hand; *shohin* is less than 10 inches (25.5 cm) high; and four-man bonsai require four people to move them. No such size categories exist in Hòn Non Bộ. Smaller displays may exist side by side with very large ones; the displays trade off adequate space for each Hòn Non Bộ against showing as many as possible. More space will be allotted to Hòn Non Bộ in gardens, but if the owner is an artist or collector, empty space is abhorred and the garden will be filled up as quickly as possible.

Initially, only wealthy people owned more than one Hòn Non Bộ, and they would display one in the front of the home and the others in the garden. Now it is possible for even skilled amateurs to have more than one. Multiple Hòn Non Bộ in a garden should be treated as a large composition and displayed with consideration for the height, scale, and overall perspective of the arrangement, keeping in mind the requirements of the various plants for light or protection from wind, sun, or rain.

The pots in which bonsai are displayed are either special pots used only for display—old Chinese pots are far too valuable to leave plants in year-round—or are cleaned very carefully before going on display. Hòn Non Bộ pots are used year-round. For display, they may be cleaned and oiled on the outside with baby oil or liquid furniture polish, but the inside of the pot is not cleaned and the water is not changed. The water is left unchanged for two reasons: dirty water is natural, and murky water prevents the bottom of the pot from being seen and so its shallowness is hidden.

Cò Bay Dưới Ánh Mặt Trời (Egrets Flying in the Sun), Lít Phan's Hòn Non Bộ interpreting the mountainous islands in Hạ Long Bay.

181

Trees and plants may be replaced if they have faded, but moss, molds, and silt remain in Hòn Non Bộ to preserve the appearance of a natural landscape. The plants are replaced with fresh greenery because the Vietnamese landscape is a lush green jungle in many places, and this lush greenness is carried over into the miniature landscapes.

Bonsai are displayed almost exclusively on stands or slabs, with the size and shape dependent on the tree and pot. Wooden slabs or sections out of a tree and low or medium stands are used to bring the plant to eye level. Tall stands are used so that the tail of the cascading plants does not touch the display table. It is particularly important to evoke the image of a tree hanging down the side of a mountain because that is how it would appear in nature. Hòn Non Bộ treats plant and tree placement as a design issue in which plants and trees may be placed at various heights on the mountain (but generally not at the top) depending on their natural setting and the desire of the artist. Stands are little used in Hòn Non Bộ. Stands that would hold a 25- to 50-pound (10 to 20 kg) bonsai would not support a 150- to 200-pound (70 to 90 kg) Hòn Non Bộ. Additionally, Hòn Non Bộ are not designed to be seen at eye level but rather are intended to be seen from the top and from all sides.

At a one-man show for the Vietnamese Medical Association, the authors discovered a new way to display Lít Phan's Hòn Non Bộ. The center of the display room had to be left open, so the Hòn Non Bo were displayed against the wall. One of the walls was covered with mirrors from the ceiling down to 30 inches (75 cm) from the floor. The mirrored background proved to be a perfect way to allow viewers to see the back of the displays even though they couldn't walk around them. Quite literally, the mirrors doubled the effect of the display.

Bonsai often appear at their best when viewed from a slight distance, and good display techniques will permit this. Hòn Non Bộ may be viewed from a distance to get the overall contours of the mountain, but often it is better to view them up close to observe the detail created by the artist. Figures the size of a peanut may not be visible from a distance but may be important in conveying what the artist was trying to represent, so observation up close may be necessary to understand the meaning of the piece.

Displays in Việt Nam

In Việt Nam, small Hòn Non Bộ or miniscenes may be placed inside the house. At temples or pagodas, Hòn Non Bộ are placed in the front of the yard or by the side of the temple. Hòn Non Bộ may also be built in an aquarium or in a pond dug in the ground or in a high-walled enclosure. Ponds (a type of container) can be round,

A Hòn Non Bộ reflected in a mirror, so allowing
viewers to see all its sides even when there is not
enough room to display it away from the wall.

semicircular, oval, hexagonal, or square. In ponds, people usually add lotus or water lilies and goldfish. Visitors to these places will be able to watch the goldfish swim in the pond while the air is filled with lotus fragrance as they stroll around to enjoy the beauty from each side.

The Vietnamese of the old days did not have clubs for Hòn Non Bộ or miniature plants. The techniques, therefore, have not been passed on in book form, and so people have acquired different tastes and use different methods of building. People may have Hòn Non Bộ built in the corners of back yards in the middle of little ponds in which goldfish swim freely. Those whose homes do not have yards build their Hòn Non Bộ for indoors.

In Việt Nam, people of all ages continue to enjoy this art. Now those who are interested in Hòn Non Bộ get together in clubs to discuss and exchange ideas and experiences. On special occasions, like Tết (the lunar New Year), people have ex-

A tiny fisherman the size of a peanut. Artists who want to do well with Hòn Non Bộ must constantly work to improve their sense of proportion.

hibitions of Hòn Non Bộ that are sometimes displayed with paintings behind them. The paintings may be of the moon, sunset, morning sun, or mountains.

Displays of Vietnamese Culture in the United States

As with bonsai in the United States, which was developed extensively in California by Japanese immigrants, Hòn Non Bộ has been developed primarily in California by Vietnamese immigrants. The first club dedicated to this art in San Diego was named the San Diego Artistic Plants and Landscape Association. Under President Lít Phan, this club was the first to show Hòn Non Bộ in San Diego.

A second club in San Diego called Hội Hòn Non Bộ (Hòn Non Bộ Association) attracts many people who love this art. The Association has held exhibitions in a number of places in Orange County, California, during the traditional Vietnamese Tết. Both annual and special exhibitions have taken place in Balboa Park in San Diego. The special events have also been televised. As a special gift, Hội Hòn Non Bộ gave a major Hòn Non Bộ to the Botanical Building in Balboa Park to introduce this symbol of the unique art of the Vietnamese to the people of the United States.

Nguyệt-Mai Đinh, Lít Phan's wife, helping to set up a display at the Chinese Cultural Center in El Monte, California.

These displays of Hòn Non Bộ are not for competition, but rather for the education and pleasure of the general public. While space limitations may require that the displays be lined up around the edge of a large room, ideally each Hòn Non Bộ should be set out away from the wall so that it can be enjoyed from all sides. A 30-inch- (75-cm-) high table may make the Hòn Non Bộ too tall to show the top of the mountain; tables ranging from 18 to 24 inches (45.5 to 61 cm) high do a better job. There is a subtle psychological difference between looking up at a mountain as compared to looking down on a mountain. The relationship between the viewer and the mountain changes when the viewer sees the mountain as a bird would rather than as a deer might.

A Nontraditional Tiểu Cảnh

The photographs of a train and train track are of a Tiểu Cảnh that show very different scenery from the high karst mountains of Việt Nam. This Tiểu Cảnh came about after a display of Hòn Non Bộ in the San Diego Model Railroad Museum in Balboa Park came to an end. John Rotsart, the executive director of the museum, and author Lít Phan collaborated and combined their skills to create a scene with a distinctly American diesel engine running on a track around the lip of the basin. A windmill was added to change the scenery even more from that of the usual landscape in Việt Nam. The resulting nontraditional display was shown at the Del Mar Fair in Del Mar, California, for three weeks, with the train running on the hour, every hour.

The Future of Hòn Non Bộ

Some experimentation is going on to determine the best height to use for feet on pots. The feet may be somewhat taller in proportion than those on bonsai pots as the concrete trays are not displayed on stands as bonsai are. The extra height keeps the tray from appearing to sit flat on a table or bench. Rules for display are still being developed.

The miniature landscape itself is still expected to meet the standards of the real world it represents. Accuracy of detail is always important when reducing a landscape to scale. For example, the approaches to a bamboo bridge should slant up to the center of the bridge, not down to it.

Two developments introduced by Lít Phan include the use of an aquarium pump to create a waterfall and the use of a mist-maker to create fog over the water. The

A nontraditional Tiểu Cảnh with a train track running
along the basin's lip and under the overhanging rocks.

Detail of a nontraditional Tiểu Cảnh showing a diesel engine
pulling several cars under the mountain's overhang.

187

Both approaches to a bamboo bridge should slope downward from its center because it is important to depict such details accurately when reducing a landscape to scale.

Innovations to traditional Hòn Non Bộ include waterfalls. A waterfall pump can be hidden behind a small- or medium-sized mountain.

equipment was not available to earlier Vietnamese artists, but now that it is available, it has been introduced to Hòn Non Bộ in Việt Nam. The Dragon Basin shown at the beginning of chapter 5 did not contain a waterfall in 1980, but one was added later. The pump should be hidden carefully behind the rocks, and the outlet leading to the waterfall is built into the rocks. The whole effect is that of a natural waterfall occurring part way down the mountain. Mist is a common feature in Việt Nam and waterfalls are spread throughout the mountainous areas.

As the Vietnamese in the United States add new scenery to their Hòn Non Bộ, and as nonVietnamese learn the art, there are likely to be changes in the shape and style of Hòn Non Bộ. This is a natural evolution; after all, within the framework of mountains, plants, and water, there are an untold number of possibilities for new Hòn Non Bộ.

One of the possibilities that will make this art form attractive to more people in the United States is the use of small ceramic trays and small mountains rather than large concrete pots with large mountains. Small trays are used in Việt Nam but usually contain only rocks and water, with no plants; most plants there are too large to be in proportion to the miniature Hòn Non Bộ. The miniature Hòn Non Bộ shown in the last few photographs of this chapter display plants commonly available in the United States. The size of these small landscapes allows them to be displayed in

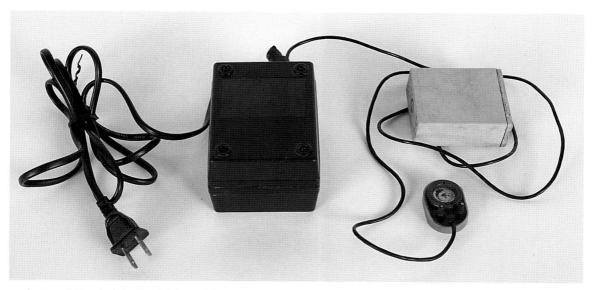

A new addition to Hòn Non Bộ is a mist-maker. It is used to create a low-lying fog that resembles the fog found over an ocean.

An 18-inch (45.5-cm) Hòn Non Bộ
by Lít Phan with a boat that was
made by his wife, Nguyệt-Mai Đinh.

Cavernous mountain that is no more than 5
inches (12.5 cm) tall. The eroded shapes are
common in the Vietnamese landscape.

190

A rare, top-heavy mountain in
the shape of a gargoyle.

Martha Altus-Buller, C.P.A., with a
miniature Hòn Non Bộ in her office.

homes and offices; the pots are Japanese *suiban* less than 12 inches (30.5 cm) long. By comparison, some of the concrete pots created for Lít Phan's Hòn Non Bộ are 40 inches (100 cm) long.

Traditionally, the Vietnamese have not used dead trees or driftwood (known to bonsai creators as *jin* and *shari*). The Tiểu Cảnh translated as "Windswept" shown in the Gallery is a departure from the tradition of using no dead or partially dead plants. The tree is a California juniper (*Juniperus californica*) estimated to be several hundred years old, with only a very fine lifeline hidden on the back of the sand-blasted trunk. This Tiểu Cảnh is an adaptation to the scenes and trees of California—a first of its kind.

Nghỉ Ngơi (Ducks at Rest)

CHAPTER TWELVE

A Gallery
of Hòn Non Bộ
and Tiểu Cảnh

As you look at the pictures in the Gallery of Hòn Non Bộ and Tiểu Cảnh, remember that the tallest mountain is only 25 inches (63 cm) tall, the longest pot is 48 inches (120.5 cm) long, and some of the figures, animal and human alike, are less than ½ inch (1 cm) tall.

Bronze drums dating from the seventh to the second century B.C., used by the leaders as a means of communication from village to village, were incised with designs representing the mystical powers of mountains and water. Rivers, trees, and stones have been revered for centuries. Like the ancient Vietnamese, the authors of this book believe that stones have near-magical qualities. Stroll through these miniature landscapes at the risk of becoming a believer yourself.

Đợi Chờ (Waiting)

Săn Mồi (Hunting)

Bình Minh Ổ Việt Nam (Morning in Việt Nam)

Hang Gió Tây (West Wind Cave)

Cuốn Theo Chiều Gió (Windswept)

Phơi Lưới (Drying the Net)

Núi In Bóng Nước (Mountain Reflections)

Quê Nhà (My Homeland)

Ông Câu (The Fisherman)

Núi Đá Treo (Hanging Mountain)

Đàn Vịt Hoang (Wild Ducks)

Đôi Nai Bên Bờ Suối (Two Deer by a Stream)

Cầu Đá (Stone Bridge)

Hòn Chim Két (Cockatiel Islands)

Cò Bay Về Núi (Egrets Returning Home)

225

Index

The character Ð does not appear in the roman alphabet. It is pronounced as a roman D. Words starting with Ð or đ appear after words starting with the roman D. The roman D as used in Vietnamese words is pronounced as a Y. Italicized page numbers refer to illustrations in the text.

accessories, 37
  animals, 47, 141–142
  birds, 47, 71, *74*, 94–95, *120*, 141–142, 147, *161–162*
  boats, *22, 30, 120*, 141, *146*, 147, *190*
  bonze, 69, 141
  bridges, *30*, 70, *70*, 100, 141–142, *143–144, 188*
  cottages and huts, *30*, 141, *146*, 147, *158, 161*
  fairies, 47
  fisherman, 141, 147
  flags and pennants, 47
  gate, *145*
  gazebo, *145*
  handmade, 127, 141–142
  jewels, 47
  pagodas and temples, 141–142, *144*, 147
  Quan Âm, *67*
  scale of, 71, 142, 157
  scholars, 141
  waiting house, *140*
  water carrier, *70*
  woodcutters, 141
Alyssum, 150, *156*
aquarium. *See* containers

baby's tears. *See Soleirolia soleirolii*
bamboo, 46–47. *See also Sasa*
banyan, 64
basins. *See* containers
Bay Dưới Ánh Mặt Trời (Egrets Flying in the Sun). *See* displays of, Hòn Non Bộ
Bể Cạn (shallow container), 46
beefwood. *See Casuarina*
Bình Minh Ở Việt Nam (Morning in Việt Nam). *See* displays of, Hòn Non Bộ
bonkei, 12
bonsai, 37, 79, 94, 130, 136, 138, 157, 180
bonze, 27, 47. *See also* accessories

boxwood. *See Buxus*

bridges. *See* accessories

Buddha, 19, 22, 25, 72, 141

Buddhism, 50, 72

bullrush, miniature. *See Typha minima*

Buxus, 133

Buxus microphylla var. *japonica*, *148*

cajeput. *See Melaleuca leucadendra*

California juniper. *See Juniperus californica*

Carex, 149, *150*

Casuarina, 58

Cat, Year of the, 48

Cầu Đá (Stone Bridge). *See* displays of, Hòn Non Bộ

caverns, 18–19, 21–26, *27*, 28, 31, 34, 72

caves. *See* caverns

cây cảnh (plants in pots), 58

Cây Kiểng (art of miniature plants), 58

ceramic. *See* containers

Châu Đốc, 18

China, 12, 17, 44–45, 51–52, 56, 142

Chinese elm. *See Ulmus parvifolia*

Chinese influence, 47, 56–58, 64, 142, 147

Chorisia speciosa, 42

Chùa Hạ ("infra pagoda"). *See* pagodas

Chùa Hương. *See* Hương Sơn

Chùa Thượng ("supra pagoda"). *See* pagodas

Chùa Trung ("mid pagoda"). *See* pagodas

cinnamon trees, 51

Cò Bay Về Núi (Egrets Returning Home). *See* displays of, Hòn Non Bộ

composition, 71, *86*, 100, 119–127, *120–125*, 131, 178

Con Chó Đá (The Stone Dog), 43

concrete, 69, 89–91, 110, *110–111*, 113–116

    containers. *See* containers

    trays. *See* containers

Confucianism, 50, 72

conifers, 129

containers, 69, 95, 98, *104*, 105–116, *113–115*, *168*, *176*, *179*, 181

    as aquarium, 106, 182

    in bonsai, 79, 95, 156, 180

    ceramic, 79, 105, 178

    concrete, 79, 84, 105, 178–179, 182

    marble, 79

    in penjing, 79, 82

    as ponds, 183–184

    stucco, 63, 69, 105

    trays, 12, 92, *130*, *131*, 186, 189

cotton rose. *See Hibiscus mutabilis*

creeds, 7, 38–39

Cuốn Theo Chiều Gió (Windswept). *See* displays of, Tiểu Cảnh

Cycas revoluta, 52

Cyperus alternifolius, 148, *149*

Cyperus alternifolius 'Gracilis', 148

Cyperus isocladus, 148–149

Đại Cồ Việt (Great Việt), 24, 43

Đại Việt (Great Việt), 52

Đà Lạt Waterfalls, 28, 30

Dancing Phoenix. *See* displays of, Hòn Non Bộ

Đàn Vịt Hoang (Wild Ducks). *See* displays of, Hòn Non Bộ

de B'haine, Pierre Joseph Georges Pigneau, 56

diamonds, 18

display, clubs for, 184–185

display, techniques in

    bonsai, 82, 177–178, 182

    Hòn Non Bộ, 177–180, *178–179*, 182–183, *183*, 190

    penjing, 82

displays of, Hòn Non Bộ

    in Balboa Park, 13, 64, *78*, *80–87*, 185, *185*

    Bay Dưới Ảnh Mặt Trời (Egrets Flying in the Sun), 179, 181

    at Bến Đục Pagoda, *40*

Bình Minh Ở Việt Nam (Morning in Việt Nam), *97–99*, 144, *200–201*

Cầu Đá (Stone Bridge), 70, 100, *101*, *220–221*

at the Chinese Cultural Center, *185*

Cò Bay Về Núi (Egrets Returning Home), *74*, *224–225*

Dancing Phoenix, *44*, 46

Đàn Vịt Hoang (Wild Ducks), *216–217*

at Den of the Kings, *57*

Đợi Chờ (Waiting), *96*, *196–197*

in Dragon Basin, Ngọc Sơn Temple, *104*

Father and Son, *91–92*, *91–92*

Garden Hòn Non Bộ, *65–68*

Hang Gió Tây (West Wind Cave), 28, *202–203*

Hòn Chim Két (Cockatiel Islands), 95, *96*, *222–223*

Nghỉ Ngơi (Ducks at Rest), *194*

at Nha Trang Oceanography Institute, *54*

Núi Đá Treo (Hanging Mountain), *214–215*

Núi In Bóng Nước (Mountain Reflections), *73*, *208–209*

Ông Câu (The Fisherman), *212–213*

Phơi Lưới (Drying the Net), *206–207*

Quê Nhà (My Homeland), *210–211*

in Sài Gòn train station, *59*

Săn Mồi (Hunting), *198–199*

Sơn Thủy Bồn Cảnh (Landscape in the Water Tank), 58

Sương Mai (A Foggy Morning), *75*, 179

in the Temple of Literacy Shrine, *45*

at the temple of Quán Thánh (Saint Mandarin), *41*

at Thái Bình Lâu (Extreme Peace Pavilion), 58

at Trấn Quốc Pagoda, *39*

displays of, Tiểu Cảnh

Cuốn Theo Chiều Gió (Windswept), 192, *204–205*

Đôi Nai Bên Bờ Suối (Two Deer by a Stream), *152*, *218–219*

in San Diego Model Railroad Museum, 186, *187*

Đoạn Trường Tân Thanh (The Story of Kiều), 54

Dog, Year of the, 52

Dog Island. *See* Hòn Con Chó

dogs, heavenly, *42–43*, 46, 72, 141

Đợi Chờ (Waiting). *See* displays of, Hòn Non Bộ

Đôi Nai Bên Bờ Suối (Two Deer by a Stream). *See* displays of, Tiểu Cảnh

Động Đình lake, 17

Động Hương Tích. *See* Hương Sơn

Dragon Descender. *See* Hạ Long Bay

dragons, 18, 26, 46, 64–65, *68*, 69, 72, *104*, 105, 141

driftwood, 192

drums, 195

Drying the Net. *See* displays of, Hòn Non Bộ

Ducks at Rest. *See* displays of, Hòn Non Bộ

dwarf horsetail. *See Equisetum hyemale*

dwarf iris. *See Iris tenuifolia*

dwarf papyrus. *See Cyperus alternifolius*

dwarf sasa bamboo. *See Sasa*

dynasties

Later Lý, 47

Lê, 26, 46–47, 52–53

Lý, 46–49, 51

Mạc Đăng Dung, 52–53

Ngô, 43

Nguyễn, 53, 56–58

North, 53

Post-Lê, 52

Pre-Lê, 45

South, 52–53

Tây Sơn, 27, 31, 56

Trần, 49–50

egrets. *See* accessories

Egrets Flying in the Sun. *See* displays of, Hòn Non Bộ

Egrets Returning Home. *See* displays of, Hòn Non Bộ

elephants, 19, 21–22

elm. *See Ulmus*

Equisetum hyemale, 149, *149*

Erodium, 150

Eternity Mountain or Mountains, 47

fairies. *See* accessories

Fansipan, 17

Father and Son. *See* displays of, Hòn Non Bộ

Father and Son Island. *See* Hòn Phụ Tử

feather stone. *See* rocks

feng shui, 64–65

Ficus, 129, 133, 135–136, *139*, *159*

Ficus benjamina, 58, 160

Ficus elastica, 58

Ficus macrophylla, *159*

Ficus religiosa, 58

Ficus retusa, 58

figures. *See* accessories

fish, 17, 46, 48, 51, *101*, 184

   in Hòn Non Bộ displays, 50, 64, 69, 106, 139, 178–179

Fisherman, The. *See* displays of, Hòn Non Bộ

Five-Element Mountain. *See* Ngũ Hành Sơn

floss silk tree. *See Chorisia speciosa*

Foggy Morning, A. *See* displays of, Hòn Non Bộ

Forbidden Citadel, 57

Fragrant Mountain. *See* Hương Sơn

French influence, 56–57

gardens, royal, 44, 49–50, 177

Giao Chỉ, 42

Giả Sơn (artificial mountain). *See* mountains

Goat, Year of the, 53

Gouga Fall, 28

grasses, 131, 157

Great Việt. *See* Đại Cồ Việt; Đại Việt

Hải Vân Pass, 28

Hạ Long Bay (Dragon Descender), *16*, 18, *19, 21*, 94

Hang Gió Tây (West Wind Cave). *See* displays of, Hòn Non Bộ

Hanging Mountain. *See* displays of, Hòn Non Bộ

Hà Tiên, 18, 30–31, *34*

Heaven-Man-Earth, 37–38

heron's bill. *See Erodium*

Hibiscus mutabilis, 42

Hoa Lư, 24–26, *24*, 138

Hòn Chim Két (Cockatiel Islands). *See* displays of, Hòn Non Bộ

Hòn Chồng, *25*

Hòn Con Chó (Dog Island), 18, *19*

Hòn Phụ Tử (Father and Son Island), 31, *32*, 89

Hồ Quý Ly, 51–52

Horse, Year of the, 53

Huế, 56–57, *57*

Hunting. *See* displays of, Hòn Non Bộ

Hương Sơn (Fragrant Mountain), 21–23

Hương Tích Pagoda, *23*

insects and pests, 138, 148–149

Iris tenuifolia, 150, *151*

jin. *See* driftwood

junipers, miniature, 58, 129, *148*

Juniperus california, 192

Juniperus chinensis 'Kishu Shimpaku', 133

Juniperus procumbens 'Nana', *128*, 131, 133, *134*

karst mountains, 95, 125, 186
Khải Thánh pavilion, 44–45

Landscape in the Water Tank. *See* displays of, Hòn Non Bộ
Lê Lợi, 52–53
limestone, 95, 101, 125
lotus, 184

mallow, 58
meditation. *See* creeds
Melaleuca leucadendra, 58
Miniscene. *See* Tiểu Cảnh
mist-maker, 186, *189*
molds, 105–107, *108–111*, 110, 114–116, 173–174
Monkey, Year of the, 45, 56
Moreton Bay fig. *See Ficus macrophylla*
Morning in Việt Nam. *See* displays of, Hòn Non Bộ
mortar, 89, 91, 105, 110–116, *111–113*, 116, *154*, 171, 174
moss, 150, 157
Mother's Milk. *See* Sữa Mẹ
Mountain Reflections. *See* displays of, Hòn Non Bộ
mountains, artificial, 93–95, *93–94*, 100, *101–102*, 107, 115, 118
   Giả Sơn (artificial mountain), 7, 40–41, 46
   Non Bộ (mountain set), 7, 40–41
   Núi Non Bộ (miniature mountain), 7, 40–41
mountain set. *See* mountains
My Homeland. *See* displays of, Hòn Non Bộ

Nam Lĩnh, 17
Nghỉ Ngơi (Ducks at Rest). *See* displays of, Hòn Non Bộ
Ngũ Hành Sơn (Five-Element Mountain), 27–28, 72
Nhà Vọng pavilion, 44–45

Ninh Bình province, 24, *24*, 26, 39, 43, *44*, 46
Nôm, 40–41, 50
Non Bộ. *See* mountains
Núi Đá Treo (Hanging Mountain). *See* displays of, Hòn Non Bộ
Núi In Bóng Nước (Mountain Reflections). *See* displays of, Hòn Non Bộ
Núi Non Bộ. *See* mountains

oil, 115, 174
Ông Câu (The Fisherman). *See* displays of, Hòn Non Bộ

pagodas, 51, 177
   Chùa Hạ ("infra pagoda"), 26
   Chùa Thượng ("supra pagoda"), 26
   Chùa Trung ("mid pagoda"), 26
   Hòn Non Nước, *50*
   Trấn Quốc Pagoda, *39*
penjing, 12, 79
phoenix, *44*, 46, 72, 141
Phơi Lưới (Drying the Net). *See* displays of, Hòn Non Bộ
Phú Quốc, 31, 48
pictographs, 48, 80
Pig, Year of the, 48
pigment. *See* concrete
pillars, carved, 48–50
pines, 58
pomegranate. *See Punica granatum*
ponds. *See* containers
pots. *See* containers
procumbens. *See Juniperus procumbens* 'Nana'
proportion, 119
pump, 103, 186, *188*, 189
Punica granatum, 155–158, 156–157

Quan Âm, 64, *67*. *See also* accessories
Quê Nhà (My Homeland). *See* displays of, Hòn Non Bộ

Red Pavilion. *See* Tử Các
rocks
    arrangement of, 93–95, *96–99*, 98–103
    cracks in, 88–89, 153
    feather stone, 89, 92, 171
    working with, 88–92, *90, 96,* 135, *172*
Rooster, Year of the, 56
Royal Elevated Garden, 52
rush. *See Scirpus cernuus*

safety gear, 171, *171*
sago palm. *See Cycas revoluta*
Săn Mồi (Hunting). *See* displays of, Hòn
    Non Bộ
Sasa, 150, *151*
Scirpus cernuus, 148, 150, *151, 161*
sedges, miniature. *See Carex*
seven palaces, 46
shan. *See* driftwood
Slabs of Pledge, 42
soil, 155–159, *159*
Soleirolia soleirolii, 136, 148
Sơn Thủ Bồn Cảnh (Landscape in the
    Water Tank). *See* displays of, Hòn
    Non Bộ
spirits, 11, 37, 42–43
stalactite, 19, 23, 25–26
Stone Bridge. *See* displays of, Hòn Non Bộ
Stone Dog, The. *See* Con Chó Đá
stone dogs, 42–43
Story of Kiều, The. *See* Đoạn Trường Tân
    Thanh
"Story of Man Nương, The" (The Lady of
    Man), 42
Sữa Mẹ (Mother's Milk), 23
suiban. *See* pots
suiseki, 79
Suối Tranh (Thatch Spring), 31
Sương Mai (A Foggy Morning). *See* dis-
    plays of, Hòn Non Bộ
symbolism, 71, 79, 84, 119, 127, 147

Tamarindus indica, 58
Tam Cương (Three Duties of Women), 72
Taoism, 50, 72
Thắng Cảnh, 48
Thatch Spring. *See* Suối Tranh
themes of Hòn Non Bộ, 71–72, 76
Thiên Phương, 58
Three Duties of Women. *See* Tam Cương
Thuja orientalis, 58
Tiểu Cảnh (miniscene), 71, 119, 153–159,
    154, 186, *187*
Tiger, Year of the, 21
Trạng Trình, 53
Trấn Quốc Pagoda. *See* pagodas
trays. *See* containers
Tử Các (Red Pavilion), 54
tufa, 95
turtles, 26, 46, 50–51, 72, 141
Typha minima, 150

Ulmus, 133, 135, *165*
Ulmus parvifolia, 137–138, 163, 166

Việt Nam
    geography, 17–35
    history of, 17–35, 42–58
Việt Sử Lược (A Summary of Việt His-
    tory), 45, 47–48

Waiting. *See* displays of, Hòn Non Bộ
water, 69, 181
waterfalls
    in Hòn Non Bộ, 68, *83, 87,* 88–89, *104,*
    105, 186, *188,* 189
    in nature, 17–18, 28, 30–31
water lilies, 184
West Wind Cave. *See* displays of, Hòn
    Non Bộ
Wild Ducks. *See* displays of, Hòn Non Bộ
Windswept. *See* displays of, Tiểu Cảnh
worship, 11, 37, 42, 49